W9-AZW-580

Drink water from your own cistern,
  running water from your own well.
How may your water sources be dispersed abroad,
  streams of water in the streets? (Prv 5:15-16)

> Words quoted by Pope Clement VIII,
> congratulating Francis de Sales in the public
> consistory of March 22, 1599, examining
> candidates for the episcopate.

May Saint Francis de Sales, the Doctor of the spiritual life, lead numerous followers on the noble and right paths which he has made easy by his apt counsels . . . May he watch over with loving vigilance the Institute of the Visitation, which he founded. May he keep under his affectionate and attentive protection the Salesian family of Don Bosco and those other families who have sought from him the principles and forms of the spiritual life.

> Pope Paul VI in his apostolic letter on Saint
> Francis de Sales in 1967, *The Gem of Savoy.*

St. Francis de Sales
Don Bosco's Patron

*St. Francis de Sales
in the Times, Life and Thought
of St. John Bosco*

by
Rev. Arnaldo Pedrini, SDB

Compiled and edited by
Francis J. Klauder, SDB

DON BOSCO PUBLICATIONS
New Rochelle, New York

Originally published as *San Francesco di Sales e Don Bosco* by Reverend Arnaldo Pedrini, SDB (Roma, 1983)

Cover painting courtesy of Rev. John Connery, OSFS, De Sales Secular Institute, Childs, Maryland

Nihil Obstat:
Joseph M. Occhio, SDB, STL, Ph.D., Censor Librorum
August 28, 1987

Imprimatur:
Most Rev. Frank J. Rodimer, D.D.
Bishop of Paterson, New Jersey
September 8, 1987

The *nihil obstat* and *imprimatur* are official declarations that a book or pamphlet is free of doctrinal or moral error. No implication is contained therein that those who have granted the nihil obstat and imprimatur agree with the contents, opinions or statements expressed.

Library of Congress Cataloging-in-Publication Data
Pedrini, Arnaldo
[*San Francesco di Sales e Don Bosco*. English]
Saint Francis de Sales, Don Bosco's patron: Saint Francis de Sales in the times, life, and thought of Saint John Bosco / compiled and edited by Francis J. Klauder.
"An adaptation from the translation of Reverend Wallace L. Cornell, SDB, of *San Francesco di Sales e Don Bosco* by Reverend Arnaldo Pedrini, SDB."
Bibliography: p.
Includes index.
1. Bosco, Giovanni, Saint, 1815-1888. 2. Christian saints–
Italy–Biography. 3. Francis, de Sales, Saint, 1567-1622–Influence.
I. Klauder, Francis J. II. Title.
BX4700.B75P3613 1988   271'.79–dc 19
[B] 87-30866

ISBN 0-89944-092-4 (pbk.)
ISBN 0-89944-096-7 (cl.)

Printed in the United States of America
91 90 89 88   5 4 3 2 1

In grateful memory of
Wallace L. Cornell
Stalwart Salesian Priest

Contents

Foreword

The volume of published works on Saint Francis de Sales is impressive and is continually expanding, giving substance to the words of Sirach as quoted in the decree *Quanto Ecclesiae* of Pius IX in 1877:

Many will praise his understanding;
  his fame can never be effaced;
Unfading will be his memory,
  through all generations his name will live;
Peoples will speak of his wisdom,
  and in assembly sing his praises. *(Sir 39:9-10)*

The author of the present book is a Salesian of Don Bosco, the great friend of young people who took much of his inspiration from Saint Francis de Sales, the Doctor of Divine Love. The author describes the growing influence of Salesian spirituality in the Church and tells in particular the story of Don Bosco's love for the saint whom he chose as patron of his multiple enterprises.

I am very happy that this work is now being made available to an English-speaking audience. The Salesian Congregation, in its many-faceted apostolate among young people throughout the world, strives to educate along the paths of the heart, in the belief, with Don Bosco, that education is first and last "a question of the heart." These words echo those of our patron, "… only the language of the heart can ever touch another heart." (O XII, 321)

It is good to see how Saint Francis de Sales, who so inspired Don Bosco, has given rise to other splendid manifestations of devotion and holiness in the Church and in the world. May this influence continue to grow, for God's greater glory.

Martin McPake, SDB
Salesian General Councillor
Rome
June 1, 1988

Editor's Preface

The year 1988 marks the first centenary of the death of Don Bosco. One of the most precious legacies that he left to his followers was the Salesian spirit. Today, as we try to recapture some of the charisma of Don Bosco, deep reflection on the Salesian spirit and its origin is not only appropriate but necessary. A few years ago Father Arnaldo Pedrini, SDB, took up this task in a book written in Italian: *San Francesco di Sales e Don Bosco*. Its purpose was to trace Don Bosco's devotion to Saint Francis de Sales, whose name and spirit he bequeathed to his followers. On the basis of this book and its translation by Father Wallace Cornell, of happy memory, the present book endeavors to show the importance of Don Bosco's connection to Francis de Sales—the Salesian connection—which prompted him to adopt not only the name Salesian but also the spirit of the saint as his own.

Using Father Pedrini's book and Father Cornell's translation as its primary source and other resource materials as available, the present work concentrates on the gradual and providential development of Don Bosco's appreciation of the gentle saint he chose as patron. There has been a change in the format of this American edition of Pedrini's book.[1] Chapters have been rearranged, materials reapportioned and comparisons added. The influence of Saint Francis de Sales on Don Bosco is seen over against the wider perspective of the vast appeal that Saint Francis de Sales has enjoyed in the Church and in society. His influence in the modern world is great.

The editor trusts that this adaptation of the Pedrini source will enhance his work, making it useful not only to the various branches of Don Bosco's large family but also to the wider gamut of Salesian families, as well as to all who continue to be fascinated with the zealous figure of the bishop of Geneva, the gentleman saint.

Francis J. Klauder, SDB, Ph.D.
Institute of Salesian Studies, Berkeley, California
January 24, 1987, Feast of Saint Francis de Sales

Heartfelt Thanks
to

Very Rev. Martin McPake, SDB
Rev. Paul Avallone, SDB
Rev. John Ayers, SDB
Rev. John Malloy, SDB
Rev. David Moreno, SDB
Rev. Joseph Occhio, SDB
Rev. Eugene M. Brown
Rev. John Connery, OSFS
Rev. Lewis Fiorelli, OSFS
Rev. Joseph Power, OSFS
Sr. Mary of the Sacred Heart Klauder, VHM
Sr. M. Gabrielle Muth, VHM
Mrs. Janice Schmitt

List of Abbreviations

Amadei: Amadei, Angelo. *Don Bosco e il suo apostolato.*

Annali: *Annali della società Salesiana.* Eugenio Ceria, ed.

ASC: *Acts of the Superior Chapter of the Salesian Society.*

Aubry: Aubry, Joseph, SDB. *The Renewal of Our Salesian Life.* 2 vols.

BM: *Biographical Memoirs of Saint John Bosco.* Rev. Diego Borgatello, SDB, ed. and trans. References beyond the fourteenth volume refer to the Italian edition. (See MB below.)

C: *Opere e scritte edite e inedite di Don Bosco.* Alberto Caviglia, ed. 6 vols.

E: *Epistolario di San Giovanni Bosco.* Eugenio Ceria, ed. 4 vols.

Giraudi: Giraudi, F. *L'Oratorio di Don Bosco.*

L: *Lettere circolari di Don Paolo Albera.*

LAS: *Opere edite di San Giovanni Bosco.* Raffaele Farina and Pietro Ambrosio, eds. 37 vols.

MB: *Memorie biografiche di Don Giovanni Bosco; Memorie biografiche del venerabile servo di Dio Don Giovanni Bosco.* G. B. Lemoyne, ed. vols. 1-9.

Memorie biografiche di S. Giovanni Bosco. G. B. Lemoyne and A. Amadei, eds. vol. 10.

Memorie biografiche del Beato Giovanni Bosco. Eugenio Ceria, ed. vols. 11-15.

Memorie biografiche di San Giovanni Bosco. Eugenio Ceria, ed. vols. 16-19.

MO: *Memorie dell'Oratorio di San Francesco di Sales dal 1815 al 1855.* Eugenio Ceria, ed.

O: *Oeuvres de Saint François de Sales: Edition d'après les autographes et les éditions originales.* 27 vols.

P: Pedrini, A. *S. Francesco di Sales e Don Bosco.*

S: Stella, Pietro. *Don Bosco: Life and Work.* Translated by John Drury. 2nd revised edition.

PART I

The Early Years

A Patron Is Found

1

Saint Francis de Sales

Don Bosco never wrote a biography of his patron, Saint Francis de Sales. He preferred to tell about his life by imitating it. Nevertheless, we do find some writings of Don Bosco about the saint and his accomplishments. His commendations of his patron are numerous, as this first chapter will show.

Don Bosco's Profile of Saint Francis de Sales

In his small volume of Church history,[2] Don Bosco has left us a brief profile of Francis de Sales (1567-1622), the saint he chose as model and patron. After stating that Francis de Sales was raised up by divine providence in that part of Savoy known as the Chablais, which was infected by teachings against the Church, Don Bosco continued:

> He is called de Sales from the place of his birth, which is a castle in Savoy. He had given himself to God from his youth and preserved his virginal purity; he had exercised himself in the practice of all the virtues, especially that of gentleness and meekness. Notwithstanding so many difficulties put in his way by his father, he renounced all the honors the world could offer him and consecrated himself to the service of the altar. Urged on by the voice of God, he performed extraordinary actions

solely with the arms of charity as he set out for the Chablais. At the sight of destroyed churches, of monasteries razed to the ground, he was all aflame with zeal and set about his apostolate. The heretics made fun of him, insulted him and tried to kill him. He persevered with patience. With his preaching and his writings and with the working of miracles, he overcame the opposition and disarmed hell, and the Catholic faith triumphed to such a degree that in a short time he led back to the fold of the Church more than 72,000 heretics in the Chablais alone. His fame of sanctity spread far and wide and, much against his will, he was created the bishop of Geneva, residing in Annecy. Here he redoubled his zeal, never refusing the most humble pastoral duties whenever the occasion arose. After a life consecrated to the greater glory of God, revered by his flock, held in high esteem by princes, loved by the popes, respected by the very heretics themselves, he rendered his soul to God at Lyons in the gardener's cottage in the Convent of the Visitation, where he had sought hospitality. It was the feast of the Holy Innocents, 1622. He was the founder of the Sisters of the Visitation, which admitted all those who, through age or infirmity, were not accepted in any other congregation.

A Saint Recommended by a Saint

In this short synopsis, Don Bosco does not mention the writings of Saint Francis de Sales, who is also a Doctor of the Church. These writings fill twenty-seven volumes. Chief among them are the *Introduction to the Devout Life* and *Treatise on the Love of God*, which Don Bosco recommended at opportune times.[3]

There is another book, not written by Don Bosco himself but republished through his initiative. This book deals with the spirit of Saint Vincent de Paul, the disciple and friend of Saint Francis de Sales. The apostolic zeal of these two saints was outstanding.[4]

It is an interesting fact that the rector of the seminary of Montpellier once asked Don Bosco whether he preferred the method of Saint Vincent de Paul or that of Saint Francis de Sales. Don Bosco answered: "You want me to explain my method . . . I don't even know it myself. I have always gone on as the Lord inspired me and the circumstances demanded." (MB XVIII, 127) Yet this very answer indicates his following of a principle of Saint Francis de Sales: "Follow, but do not anticipate, the steps of divine providence."

The love of Don Bosco for Saint Francis de Sales is rooted in the radical identity of the apostolic zeal which animated the hearts of the two saints. Imitation is the most expressive proof of love and devotion.

Don Bosco, who is the patron saint of the Catholic press, was prolific in the number of writings authored or published by him; yet he neither wrote a biography of his patron saint nor engaged in theoretical writings. Much like an editor, he knew how to make good use of material that was available, whenever he judged it conducive to the glory of God. On the other hand, Saint Francis de Sales, who is the patron of journalists, wrote extensively on doctrinal matters. Don Bosco employed the saint's writings in fulfilling his own mission.

In the introduction to the *Salesian Constitutions*, composed between 1874 and 1878, Don Bosco extracted from the rules written by Saint Francis de Sales for the Visitation Order of Sisters. In writing the rules for his Salesians, Don Bosco naturally turned to his patron, whose spirit he wished to infuse into his own society.

A pamphlet, *A Christian Vade-Mecum* (1858)—a work typical of Don Bosco in style and content—is another link with Saint Francis de Sales. In the preface he says expressly that besides the Fathers of the Church he made use of several sacred authors, such as Saint Charles Borromeo, Saint Philip Neri and Saint Francis de Sales. In three different places he advises the reading of the *Introduction to the Devout Life*, and in the section entitled "Some Advice to Young People" there are references to part three, chapter eight of the *Introduction*, as well as other passing references.

From an available collection of the *Maxims of Saint Francis de Sales*, Don Bosco included forty of them in his 1885 edition of the *Companion for Youth* (first published in 1847). Frequently these are adaptations or rewordings of the original statements of Saint Francis, such as the following: "It is a stroke of good luck for a young person to have someone to follow him up, because at that age self-love really blinds the reason." In the same *Companion for Youth* there is a meditation on heaven which contains many of the ideas and concepts found in part one, chapter sixteen of the *Introduction*.

Another book, *Il Cattolico Provveduto*, a manual of practices of piety, was compiled by Father Bonetti, one of Don Bosco's early Salesians. It contains a number of phrases and thoughts adapted from Saint Francis de Sales and a lengthy extract from part three, chapter thirty-three of the *Introduction*.

As evidenced by his letters and by the record of the *Biographical Memoirs*, Don Bosco often employed expressions and sentiments similar to those of Saint Francis de Sales. For example: "I am afraid to lose in a quarter of an hour that kindness and gentleness that I was able to store up, drop by drop, like dew, in the vessel of my heart over a period of twenty years . . ." (E IV, 205)[5] This expression was attributed to Francis de Sales by Don Bosco while he was writing a letter. His source was probably a current biography.

In the *Biographical Memoirs* we read the following saying of Don Bosco: ". . . Do not forget the importance of gentleness in our actions; win over the hearts of the young by means of love; remember that saying of Francis de Sales: 'More flies are caught with a cup of honey than with a barrel of vinegar.'" (BM XIV, 404) These words were often on the lips of Don Bosco, even if he changed them slightly at times; sometimes we find "drops" or "spoonsful" of honey or even "a plate of honey." In another place we read in a "Good Night" given by Don Bosco: "I would like you to learn how to make honey as the bees do. Do you know how they go about it? . . . they go from flower to flower to extract nectar, and only nectar." (BM VII, 366)

Don Bosco's own way of acting often expressed the thought and spirit of Saint Francis de Sales better than any quotation drawn from the saint's voluminous writings. One would have to say that Don Bosco held Francis de Sales in the highest possible esteem, not only as a person but as a saint. He enthusiastically attributed to him "holiness combined with wisdom in the way of going about things" and "a keen intellect" and called him a "great saint." Besides recognizing him as a Doctor of the Church and an outstanding figure in the field of theology and ascetics, he spoke of him as "an admirable patron," "dear and meek," "a wise educator of hearts." (cf. MB XVI, 437; P 125) A model to imitate, Saint Francis de Sales is universally acknowledged as the saint of meekness and patience.

Don Bosco loved the saint dearly, and his love was manifested by his life of dedication and immolation which made him another Francis de Sales in his own time. In him we have a beautiful "ascetical photography," the good and paternal image of the bishop of Geneva. In a dream on May 9, 1879, he saw "a man who looked like Saint Francis de Sales," whose face radiated kindness. Besides his holiness, enlivened by gentleness, Don Bosco was inspired by his doctrine and his thought. It is in this that Saint Francis de Sales is worthy of the highest glorification by the Church: he was an admirable doctor, famous for "his many writings, free from any trace of error, full of sound doctrine and full of the deepest piety." (*Salesian Bulletin*, January 1878) To know him was to love him; to honor him was for Don Bosco a recognition of his spiritual grandeur.

A Common Motto

The Salesian coat of arms forms a very important connection between the spirit of Don Bosco and that of Saint Francis de Sales. As far back as December 8, 1855, Don Bosco used the design of this emblem in one of his circular letters. On the shield is depicted a flaming heart and a representation of Francis de Sales. Beneath this is the motto: *Da mihi animas; coetera tolle* ("Give me souls; take away the rest.") The predilection Don Bosco had for this motto, which he adopted right from the beginning of his work, is well known. He attributed the motto without hesitation to his patron, expressly calling it "a motto that already belonged to Saint Francis de Sales." We know as well that when young Dominic Savio met the wise educator for the first time (October 1854), he was able to read and understand— after a few words of explanation—the Salesian motto, which hung on the saint's wall: "[Don Bosco] decorated the walls with several inscriptions which he had printed on cardboard. One was the motto of Saint Francis de Sales, *Da mihi animas; coetera tolle*, which at the time of his priestly ordination he had taken as his own. He remained faithful to it until death, for he never desired anything but to save as many souls as possible." (BM II, 410)

L'Arco has justly said: ". . . the motto *Da mihi animas*, which sums up admirably the pastoral vision of the saintly educator, Don Bosco adapted from Saint Francis de Sales. And how easy it is to recognize in this expression the style of the Doctor of Love." (P 119)

Don Bosco adapted it, we agree, to suit his personal needs. He had this motto from the very time of his preparation for sacred Orders and may have learned it from his spiritual director, Father Joseph Cafasso. In the manuscripts of Cafasso's sermons, we find the phrase expressed in this way: "Give me souls—we repeat with the apostle of charity who was Saint Francis de Sales—give me, O Lord, souls to save." (Cafasso, Don Joseph. *Manuscripts*, vol. VII, 2896)

As an intermediate source we can go back to the texts of two famous writers, Collot (died 1741) and the curate of Saint Sulpice (died 1874). Both draw upon the oral witness of Jean Pierre Camus, bishop of Belley and close friend of Francis de Sales. Although the motto was not on the latter's episcopal heraldry, Camus relates that it was an utterance frequently on his lips, expressive of his zeal for souls and so much a part of his spirit. This is confirmed by the co-foundress of the Visitation Order, Jane Frances de Chantal, who testified in the process of beatification of Francis de Sales that his constant concern was for the salvation of souls. A testimony similar to this was made by Blessed Michael Rua regarding Saint John Bosco: "He took no step, pronounced not a single word, put his hand to no task which did not involve the salvation of the young . . . With deeds and not only words he proclaimed: *Da mihi animas, coetera tolle!*" (*Lettere circolari di Don Michele Rua*; letter of January 29, 1896, Torino, 1910.) Both de Sales and Don Bosco lived in action the Salesian motto: Give me souls!

2

The Name Salesian

The Salesians of Saint John Bosco (SDB) form the third largest group of religious in the Church, after the Jesuits and Franciscans. Their initials distinguish them and set them off from other religious. For there are various congregations and institutes, as we will see later, which were founded in or around the nineteenth century and which have adopted the name of Saint Francis de Sales or have drawn their inspiration and spirituality from him.

It was Don Bosco's intuition, after placing the society which he founded under the protection of Mary Help of Christians, to name it after Saint Francis de Sales, "the zealous pastor and doctor of charity," as article nine of the revised *Salesian Constitutions* points out. Article seventeen of the same *Constitutions* is even more precise, stating that both the name and spirit of Don Bosco's society is "inspired by the optimistic humanism of Saint Francis de Sales," firmly believing in "man's natural and supernatural resources without losing sight of his weakness."

A Name Dear to All

The name of the Salesian Congregation warrants a treatise by itself. It spells out both the vast compass of Don Bosco's works and the gentle manner in which he performed them—distinct characteristics of the holy Doctor of Love. This is why Don Bosco was attracted to him and drew his inspiration from him. The name Sales, and as a consequence the title of Salesian, was certainly full of meaning for the founder, and he never tired of stressing this fact. We should not be surprised, then, to know that Don Bosco was in the habit of calling his Salesians "Sons of Saint Francis de Sales." He did this in his letters to individuals or communities but more often in his familiar talks with them. (E I, 473; II, 349) This practice was confirmed in one of his later dreams. We refer here to the dream the saint had in 1887 which foretold the future mission of the Salesians and, in particular, their devotion to the Eucharist. Don Bosco was told: "It is the wish of God and the Blessed Virgin Mary that the Sons of Saint Francis de Sales should open a house at Liege in honor of the Blessed Sacrament." (MB XVIII, 438; see also XVII, 301)

It was by a deliberate choice that Don Bosco gave the name Salesian to his society—a choice that the passing of years and subsequent events have proved to be a happy one. Don Paul Albera, second successor of Don Bosco, makes some opportune comments in this regard in two of his circular letters:

> All will benefit from realizing that they are known as Salesians which, in itself, covers a whole program and is the most efficacious incitement to walk in the footsteps of that great man whom we are proud to call our father and founder. (L 213)

> . . . Speaking of gentle kindness, can we ever forget the name which we are privileged to bear, the name of Salesians? This is a name which is widely known all over the world and is loved by all. This reminds us why our father and founder, not without good reason, chose Saint Francis de Sales as the protector of the society which he was planning to set up. With his deep understanding of human nature, he understood right from the beginning that in those times in which he was working it was essential to gain entry to hearts to do good. Therefore he pondered deeply and lovingly the words and example of that great master and model of gentle kindness and tried to walk in his footsteps. (ibid., 315)

A famous Salesian author and interpreter of Don Bosco, Father Caviglia, claimed that the first and authentic Salesian was Don Bosco himself. He turned to the saintly bishop of Geneva and drew his inspiration from him, both as regards the practice of the apostolic life and the gentle approach of his teachings. This statement is supported by the authoritative voice of Don Paul Albera in his circular letter of 1922, on the occasion of the third centenary of the death of Saint Francis de Sales:

> We who take from him not only his name but his spirit have an obligation to lead the way in celebrating this centenary worthily. Divine providence certainly had a special reason for seeing that our congregation should bear his name, rather than that of the founder; we may even presume that Don Bosco was enlightened from on high in choosing this saint as the patron of

his work and so gave his sons the name of Salesians, even though he made no mention of this in his talks or even in his memoirs. (L 552)

More Inspiration Than Dependence

Don Bosco certainly was a devotee, a great admirer of the saint of gentle kindness. From the beginning of his ecclesiastical and priestly formation, he was enthralled with this aspect or characteristic of the saint. (cf. S 253) He was also familiar with his writings, especially his masterpieces: the *Introduction to the Devout Life* and the *Treatise on the Love of God.* He certainly had read his life.

Here three questions arise: How original was Don Bosco in his ministry and his writings? How much did he borrow from Saint Francis de Sales? To what extent was he inspired by the spirit of the saint who was proposed and chosen as patron and model? It seems that it is a matter of inspiration rather than dependence.

Don Bosco did not merely adopt the name of Saint Francis de Sales out of pure convenience or ritual etiquette; on the other hand, he did not wish to limit himself to one particular spirituality. He took from Francis's writings what he considered to be the essential guidelines for the religious or ascetical life, using some of the saint's ideas and building around them. He turned to him and drew on his spirit of genial intuition. A kind of inspiration led him to fasten on the idea of love, a sublime and fundamental element of Francis's teaching, and to use it as the basis of his pastoral and educational approach, adding to it the imprint of his own personality.

Lemaire, one of the best interpreters of the thought and spirituality of Saint Francis de Sales, comments: "The bishop of Geneva is perhaps the first person to construct a whole edifice of the spiritual life based on love . . . No spirituality before was so strongly based on the driving force of love. To be more exact, for Saint Francis de Sales, love is the beginning, the means and the ends of perfection." (P 15)

Don Bosco made his own this concept of the primacy of love by his clear understanding of it and his natural and practical commonsense approach. He applied it more and more specifically as he became convinced that his apostolate was to be with the young. He looked to the spirit of Saint Francis de Sales and from it he created his own spirituality. In the words of Father Valentini: "We may say that the *spirit* of Don Bosco is the spirit of Saint Francis de Sales, but the *spirituality* of Don Bosco is not the same as that of bishop of Geneva. The spirituality of Don Bosco is a new spirituality which, although it belongs to the Salesian school, has its own specific characteristics which give it a right to be considered separately." (ibid.) Over and over again we find the same testimony.

The great educator of the young found in Saint Francis de Sales a model for his apostolic activity and for the practice of his educational method. In the service of the young, whose souls he felt called to save, he proposed Saint Francis de Sales as a model of kindness and charity. He saw in him and in his teaching a valuable guide. He was deeply grateful for this inspiration and stressed devotion to the saint throughout his life. The setting up of the first oratory and later the congregation bearing the saint's name were the chief and most meaningful gestures of that devotion. He thus erected a permanent monument that would reverence the name and foster the spirit of Saint Francis de Sales. All these facts, seen collectively, point to an appropriate and carefully-considered choice, even though certain external aspects do not seem to support this assertion. Some of Don Bosco's ideas at times run counter to those of Francis, and yet in these two men there was a marvelous convergence of thought and an identity of goals. One could almost call them spiritual twins, even though separated in time by more than two centuries.

Many Differences but One and the Same Spirit

One lived in the sixteenth and seventeenth centuries, when the Counter-Reformation was at its height, and the other lived in the mid-nineteenth century. These were two totally different epochs as far as the socio-cultural environment is concerned, and yet each age played a role in the plan of God. Both saints were men of their own times, with the characteristics proper to their family backgrounds.

In many ways these men were very different. Francis belonged to a noble family, while John came from peasant stock. One was accustomed to a comfortable lifestyle, while the other came from a beleaguered family. One had every opportunity to frequent centers of learning and culture; the other was deprived of almost every opportunity and challenged by opposition within his own family as he sought the appropriate education that would enable him to reach the goal God had set for him. Francis carried out his work as a member of the nobility and was further adorned with the dignity of a bishop. Don Bosco was a simple priest; he dressed in a threadbare cassock and worked almost exclusively with the poorer elements of society.

Francis de Sales was by nature, and still more by social status, dignified in his bearing and elegant in manner. Don Bosco had to cope with numerous disadvantages and experienced many painful misunderstandings among the clergy. The bishop of Geneva, because of his long contact with the upper classes, was predisposed to mix with the powerful, the noble and the educated; he was prepared, by his background, to be on cordial terms with all, including women. The priest from Valdocco seemed somewhat timid and introspective, hesitating to go outside the circle of his close friends and reluctant to get involved in external or civil affairs, especially politics. It was only the circumstances in which he found himself that eventually forced him to act otherwise. An innate sense of modesty led him to turn back the offer of honors, nor did he think that God had called him to work with girls. Yet all his life as a priest he visited the homes of noble families to meet benefactors, many of them ladies, without whose help he could not have carried on his work.

Leaving aside these obvious differences, Francis de Sales and Don Bosco had much in common. Nature and grace had made them complete human beings in heart and mind. Both men were able to win over souls by their gentle approach and by their fine qualities of heart and mind; they were living examples of Christian virtue. Both men had the exuberance of youth, even in their later years. Both were strong characters, even quick-tempered, who could be rather blunt at times. Yet they were able to gain control over their natures, stifling all impulsive outbursts that might be hurtful to souls. Both men were endowed with superior intelligence, a spirit of initiative and a prodigious memory which helped them to become masters in both ecclesiastical and secular learning.

An amazing array of virtues and gifts made Saint Francis de Sales the most courteous of saints. The same qualities enabled Don Bosco to be an outstanding friend and patron of young people. In Saint Francis de Sales we admire the devout and optimistic humanism which made him such an approachable and beloved person. In Don Bosco there shone forth an evangelical serenity which conquered hearts and led young people to the heights of virtue. The words of one of Don Bosco's contemporaries give us some idea of the esteem in which he was held by his fellow clergy: "In Don Bosco, Francis de Sales seemed alive in our midst. In him we could admire a shining example of every virtue . . . He was our brother who excelled in piety, gentleness and holiness . . . Just to hear him speak was enough to enkindle the flames of divine love, and it was enough to see him to feel the need to practice every virtue." (P 18)

Article twenty-one of the revised *Salesian Constitutions* makes the observation: "We study and imitate him [Don Bosco], admiring in him a splendid blending of nature and grace. He was deeply human, rich in the qualities of his people, open to the realities of this earth; and he was deeply the man of God, filled with the gifts of the Holy Spirit and living as seeing Him who is invisible."

An almost identical appraisal could be made of Saint Francis de Sales, whose spiritual affinity led Don Bosco to choose him as patron. He took the name of Salesian because of his admiration for the Doctor of Divine Love. In the holy bishop of Geneva, Don Bosco admired above all else the untiring zeal of his apostolic activity. He saw in him a model to imitate for the good of souls: a model of gentle kindness and pleasing manners, an example of the total giving of self, expressed in the motto, "Give me souls!" He was a man inspired by love in all that he did.

The close and vital affinity between the two saints is seen in the way they practiced every virtue. Besides the spirituality garnered from reading Francis's works, Don Bosco patterned his own way of acting on that of the saint from Savoy.

The reinterpretation of Salesianity made by Don Bosco bears a style unique to himself, with all the hallmarks of his genial powers of adaptation, particularly as regards the concrete application of the Preventive System. In this sense we can call Salesianity a charism of Don Bosco, although in many respects the charisms of these two saints coincide. In them we find a perfect symphony: two different persons, but one ideal which may be summed up as a search for souls and personal holiness, all for the love and greater glory of God.

In the next chapter we will ascertain how well Saint Francis de Sales was known in the nineteenth century, especially in Don Bosco's native Piedmont and in the city of Turin. We will then examine to what degree Don Bosco promoted devotion to the saint and set him up as a model. Father Philip Rinaldi, third successor of Don Bosco, whose own cause for beatification has been introduced, was convinced that the more we understand Don Bosco's relationship to Saint Francis de Sales, the more we will understand Don Bosco himself.[6]

3

The Saint from Savoy

Events in the Light of Providence

Over two centuries separated Don Bosco from Saint Francis de Sales, and yet they complemented each other. In the singular and providential plan of God, they shared the same ideals and enjoyed a spiritual affinity by which their goals and their response to God's call were identical. Is it possible that Don Bosco turned to the saint—and was so inspired by him—by mere chance? Don Paul Albera did not think so. In his circular letter, *Don Bosco Our Model*, Father Albera wrote:

Certain human deliberations and events, considered in themselves, do not seem to have any special significance; but if we look closely at them in the light of divine providence, they appear beautifully and wisely coordinated for carrying out the designs of God in the government of humanity. Don Bosco, whether acting on someone else's advice or for any other reason, chose Saint Francis de Sales as the patron of his work . . . At first glance this, as many other events in the life of Don Bosco which seemed to happen by chance, gives no impression of the extraordinary, but considered in the light of providence, it seems to indicate that Don Bosco's mission in our own days is a reflection or, better, a continuation of that initiated three centuries ago by Francis de Sales. (L 522-523)

The first providential link that connects Don Bosco to Saint Francis de Sales is the devotion to the saint from Savoy that flourished at the time of Don Bosco's birth in his native Piedmont. At that time, Piedmont, like Savoy, was one of the Sardinian states.

A Saint from Savoy

Francis de Sales, born in 1567 at Thorens, near Annecy in Savoy, never tried to disguise his justifiable pride in his birthplace. He used to say quite openly: "I am a true Savoyard, and I would not know how to be anything else."

By nationality he was neither a Frenchman nor an Italian but belonged to the province of Savoy. In 1602 he withstood pressure from the court of Paris to take up residence there and be invested with the highest ecclesiastical honors. Likewise, despite his long stay in Italy while he studied at Padua and then in Turin, where he attended to affairs of state at the court of Duke Charles Emmanuel I, Francis de Sales always boasted that he was a Savoyard. When he returned to his dear native place, it was with a sense of homesickness. This was especially true of Annecy, which was the cradle of his beloved Order of the Visitation. (Some years after the founding of the first convent, another Visitation convent, supervised by Mother Chantal herself, was built in Turin, the capital of the states of Sardinia. The sisters eventually transferred from Turin to Moncalieri, where they still treasure a precious relic: an authentic painting of the saint done in 1618, a gift of the mother foundress.)

We must not forget how much the saint felt in his heart that he was a debtor to Italian art and culture, which he had assimilated especially by his visits to various cities of Italy. Yet if Padua was the center for his intellectual formation through the study of law in the university of that city, Turin was the city dearest to his heart—it was a second home. Here was the residence of the dukes of Savoy, from whom he enjoyed the respect due to a nobleman. He visited this royal city frequently on missions of diplomacy and was a friend of Duke Charles Emmanuel, who made him welcome at the court. Because of the apostolic work Francis had done in the difficult mission of the Chablais (1594-1598), the duke used to speak proudly of him as the "Charles Borromeo" of his states.

The memory of Francis de Sales is still preserved in several cities of Piedmont, as an apostle and writer who had been, at some time, their guest. He used to stop over at Novara and Vercelli, albeit briefly, to pay his respects at the altar and sacred remains of Blessed Bernard of Mentone (also from Chambéry) and of Blessed Amadeo IX of Savoy; he greatly desired to spread devotion to the latter beyond the territory of Vercelli and Piedmont. The city of Chieri glories in the fact that Francis stayed there for some time during 1622 at the Dominican Sisters' Convent of Saint Margaret. The nuns still treasure certain objects touched by the saint and retain copies of many of his talks and conferences, which they later used as spiritual reading. The monastery where he lived has been all but pulled down or employed for other purposes, but the visitor's lodge was handed over in time to the Salesians, who used the church and part of the building as a site for a flourishing oratory. Father Barberis considered this a happy coincidence.

At Carmagnola and Saluzzo is kept alive the memory of the very close friendship of Francis de Sales with Juvenal Ancina, who was consecrated a bishop at the same time as Francis. There is a painting of the two in the cathedral of Saluzzo. On one occasion, Bishop Ancina greeted his friend with the words: *Tu vere Sal es* ("You are really salt"), alluding to his name of Sales, to which Francis promptly replied:

Tu Sal et Lux es ("You are both salt and light"), referring to the name of his See, a combination of the words *sal* and *lux*. Don Bosco remembered this in a letter to Salesian missionary Father Costamagna on January 31, 1881.

Francis de Sales made a devotional stopover at the Marian shrine of Vicoforte near Mandovi in 1603, where he left his pilgrim's staff as a devout homage. In 1622 he visited Pinerolo to preside over the Cistercian Chapter at the request of Pope Gregory XV. Perhaps one of the places in Piedmont most dear to Francis was the private chapel of the Holy Shroud, together with the Shrine of the Consolata, then served by the above-mentioned Cistercian monks. In the final period of his life, laid low by a fever and by severe illness, he spent about three months as the very welcome guest of these same monks. Instead of living at the court, where the princes and princesses of Savoy would have been delighted to give him a royal welcome, he preferred to stay in the humble quarters of a hermitage dedicated to Mary. "Let me have the consolation," he requested, "of living in your midst as a brother, because that is what I really am. Here in the presence of the virgin, the Mother of Consolation, I could not be in better company." (*Année Sainte*, VI, 167)

As soon as he felt better, Francis said farewell to Turin. In September 1622, he returned to Annecy. Three months later, on December 28, he died in the city of Lyons.

Since there were so many memories of Francis de Sales in Piedmont, his name was well known there. This was true in January 1860, the time of the ceding of the duchy of Savoy to France. In the early years of Don Bosco's life, the influence of Saint Francis de Sales in Piedmont was still considerable.

A Renowned Author

Perhaps another factor should be taken into account. It was in Turin that the *Introduction to the Devout Life*, published for the first time in Lyons in August 1608, was printed in its Italian version. Through the *Introduction* and his other writings, Francis came to be known and loved. Several biographies of the saint were also in circulation. In Turin and other Italian cities, various confraternities of both priests and lay people, founded in honor of saints or under their protection, were flourishing. In Rome there were two outstanding men, Storaci and Polidori, who became respectively the confessor and spiritual director of the seminarian and priest, John Mastai Ferretti—the future Pius IX. They established a Salesian cenacle of priests whose main aim was to live the priestly ideal more intensely, according to the doctrine and thought of Saint Francis de Sales. It is well known that Pius IX, as pope, used to read passages from the works of the saint, in accordance with the regulations of that confraternity.

Devotion to Saint Francis de Sales also flourished in many other Italian cities and regions. According to Father Stella, ". . . in Genoa, Bologna, Venice and elsewhere . . . there was the Association of Saint Francis de Sales for the defense and preservation of the faith." (S 241)

Piedmont and the city of Turin, from the very beginning of the eighteenth century, were centers of interest in Saint Francis de Sales. The dominant figure of this period was Blessed Valfre, a famous devotee of Francis. Specifically, the traditions governing the successful running of various associations were preserved.

In Turin it was not only priests, theologians and ecclesiastical students who were interested in Saint Francis de Sales and his spirituality, but also eminent personages, cultured men and women. In the house of the counts of Cavour, the picture of the Savoyard saint occupied a place of honor and privilege. All who belonged to that noble Piedmontese family, among whom the count of Cavour held pride of place, boasted of the fact that the family descended, on the paternal side, from the lords of the castle of Sales. Don Bosco was aware of this. When he heard of the death of the eminent statesman of that name, he recalled his kindness to the oratory and told the boys at the "Good Night":

> We must indeed feel pity for Count Cavour. In his last moments he did not have one sincere friend of his soul. Let us hope, however, that through the intercession of Saint Francis de Sales—a relative on his mother's side—God may have touched his heart in time and had mercy on him. (BM VI, 575-576)

Various chapels scattered throughout Turin testify to the popular devotion to the holy bishop of Geneva. Books of

Salesian maxims were very much in vogue; there were dozens of them in print, and many had gone through several editions. It is easy to understand why Don Bosco inserted these maxims in the last edition of *The Companion of Youth*, which he published in 1885.

In the Chieri Seminary and at the *Convitto*

There are two centers which promoted the memory and veneration of the bishop of Geneva in a very special way and popularized devotion to him. These were the regional seminary of Chieri and the Pastoral Institute in Turin (the *Convitto*, founded in 1817). Both of these centers for the formation of seminarians and priests were dedicated to and placed under the protection of Saint Francis de Sales and Saint Charles Borromeo, in order to put before the young men the figures of these two outstanding pastors of the Counter-Reformation.

Situated next door to the seminary at Chieri was the Church of Saint Philip, where a confraternity founded in the seventeenth century in honor of the saint from Savoy was still active. The archives of this church contain records of the various confraternities established there, including the Association of Saint Francis de Sales. (cf. S 76) This type of association, together with current lives of the saint and his writings and maxims, kept alive the memory of the bishop of Geneva in Chieri and its environs, where John Bosco studied as a seminarian. This initial contact was deepened when, after his ordination, he took up further studies at the *Convitto* in Turin.

In Don Bosco's time there were two especially worthy priests at the *Convitto*: Father Aloysius Guala and Father Joseph Cafasso, the head of the institute. They were outstanding for their learning and piety and were attracted to the Salesian concept of spirituality, the driving force of which is love. The qualities in Father Cafasso which most impressed Don Bosco were his gentleness, serenity, optimism and spirit of reconciliation. He had learned these traits from Saint Francis de Sales, to whom he was very devoted. He was greatly sought after for his ministry in the confessional and for spiritual direction. One of his biographers relates how he gave special importance to the feast of this saint, which he called "our" feastday. Another states that the spirit of Francis pervaded all his spirituality. Together with the moral teachings of Saint Alphonsus, Don Cafasso passed on this spirituality to his students, prominent among whom was John Bosco.

Father Cafasso lived at the Pastoral Institute between 1840 and 1860. In those decades there was a revival of interest in the works of Saint Francis de Sales both in France and in Italy. Cafasso had read them and found the ideas very close to his own viewpoint. He was convinced that this saint was particularly suited to modern times, when people are more easily influenced by a spirit of love and hope than by harshness and fear. He understood that it was more efficacious to pour the wine and oil of the Good Samaritan on the wounds of the soul, using an approach so favored by Saint Francis de Sales.[7]

This was the environment which influenced the young priest Don Bosco when he was invited by his saintly confessor and fellow-countryman to stay on in Turin at the Pastoral Institute. He was forever grateful for the guidance he received in those early years of his priesthood, when he intensified his priestly formation and gained practical experience. He wrote: "Don Cafasso was my guide and my spiritual director for six years. And if I have been able to do anything worthwhile, I owe it to that worthy priest into whose hands I entrusted all my deliberations, all my studies and all my activities in life." (MO 123)

It is impossible to evaluate too highly the extraordinary influence this holy priest of Castelnuovo had over Don Bosco. His example and firm direction were an inspiration to him, especially during the long years of preparation for his mission. This feeling of gratitude for this man of God was not only expressed by Don Bosco himself but also by one of his spiritual sons, John Cagliero:

> We love and hold in veneration our dear father and founder Don Bosco, but our love is great also for Saint Joseph Cafasso, who was Don Bosco's guide and advisor not only in his spiritual life but in the work he did for over twenty years. We can say indeed that the virtues, the works and the wisdom of Don Bosco are due to the influence of Don Cafasso. Let us recall that he said so

often: "It was out of obedience that I stayed on in Turin, and it was because of his direction and support that I began to gather together the first boys of the Oratory of Saint Francis de Sales." (P 36-37)

The obedience of Don Bosco to the wise direction of Father Joseph Cafasso bore great fruit in the Church for the Christian education of youth.

4

Saint Francis de Sales, Don Bosco's Personal Choice of Patron

Divine Finesse

Father Pietro Stella is one of the most highly-respected students of the history and religious environment of the times in which Don Bosco lived and worked. He expressly states that the choice of Saint Francis de Sales as a patron was a decisive event in the life of Don Bosco. (cf. S 107) The circumstances of the choice may appear to have been casual, but such was not the case. In the light of available documents and actual events, it is clear that lofty motives prompted Don Bosco to create a work and a congregation in honor of the bishop of Geneva. In considering how he was led to place himself and his work under the protection of Saint Francis de Sales, we can detect a divine finesse. This is not surprising, because many seemingly accidental events in the life of Don Bosco proved later to be providential. His followers were well aware of this. One of his early companions, Father Ruffino, wrote in his *Cronache dell'Oratorio*:

> The outstanding gifts which stood out in Don Bosco, the extraordinary events surrounding his life which we all admired so much, his unique way of leading young people along the path of virtue, the great future which he foresaw for his work were all clear evidence of the supernatural and led us to be convinced that the oratory had a glorious future ahead of it. (P 39)

The First Dream

Long before coming to know Saint Francis de Sales, Don Bosco had already received his mission from on high in a dream he had at the age of nine. That heavenly message spelled out in precise terms the mission that would be entrusted to him and the spirituality that should characterize it. It was the same as that which inspired Saint Francis de Sales. Don Bosco relates:

When I was about nine years old I had a dream that left a profound impression on me for the rest of my life. I dreamed that I was near my home, in a very large playing field where a crowd of children was having fun. Some were laughing, others were playing and not a few were cursing. I was so shocked at their language that I jumped into their midst, swinging wildly and shouting at them to stop. At that moment a Man appeared, nobly attired, with a manly and imposing bearing. He was clad with a white, flowing mantle and his face radiated such light that I could not look directly at him. He called me by my name and told me to place myself as leader over those boys, adding the words:

"You will have to win these friends of yours, not with blows but with gentleness and kindness. So begin right now to show them that sin is ugly and virtue beautiful."

Confused and afraid, I replied that I was only a boy and unable to talk to these youngsters about religion. At that moment the fighting, shouting and cursing stopped and the crowd of boys gathered about the Man who was now talking. Almost unconsciously I asked:

"But how can you order me to do something that looks so impossible?"

"What seems so impossible you must achieve by being obedient and by acquiring knowledge."

"But where, how?"

"I will give you a teacher under whose guidance you will learn and without whose help all knowledge becomes foolishness."

"But who are you?"

"I am the Son of her whom your mother has taught you to greet three times a day."

"My mother told me not to talk to people I don't know, unless she gives me permission. So please tell me your name."

"Ask my mother."

At that moment I saw beside him a lady of majestic appearance, wearing a beautiful mantle glowing as if bedecked with stars. She saw my confusion mount; so she beckoned me to her. Taking my hand with great kindness she said: "Look!"

I did so. All the children had vanished. In their place I saw many animals—goats, dogs, cats, bears and a variety of others.

"This is your field, this is where you must work," the lady told me. "Make yourself humble, steadfast and strong. And what you will see happen to these animals you will have to do for my children."

I looked again; the wild animals had turned into as many lambs, gentle, gamboling lambs, bleating a welcome for that Man and lady.

At this point of my dream I started to cry and begged the lady to explain what it all meant because I was so utterly confused. She then placed her hand on my head and said: "In due time everything will be clear to you."

After she had spoken these words, some noise awoke me; everything had vanished. I was completely bewildered. Somehow my hands still seemed to ache and my cheeks still stung because of all the fighting. Moreover, my conversation with that Man and lady so disturbed my mind that I was unable to sleep any longer that night.

In the morning I could barely wait to tell about my dream. When my brothers heard it, they burst out laughing. I then told my mother and grandmother. Each one who heard it gave it a different interpretation.

. . . I could never get that dream out of my head. What I am about to relate may give some new insight to it. I never brought up the matter and my relatives gave no importance to it. But in 1858, when I went to Rome to confer with the pope about the Salesian Congregation, Pius IX asked me to tell him everything that might have even only the slightest bearing on the supernatural. Then for the first time I told him the dream that I had when I was nine. The pope ordered me to write it in detail for the encouragement of the members of the congregation, for whose sake I had gone to Rome. (BM I, 95-96)

If we were to comment on this first dream in detail, it would be easy to collate all the aspects of the future Salesian work: from gentleness to religious instruction, from humility to fortitude, from scholarship to devotion to Mary, all culminating in a zeal and a charity that knows no limits.

Even in this simple enumeration, we can see all the characteristics of the spirituality of Saint Francis de Sales. Yet at this age John Bosco most likely did not even know the name of the gentle saint.

Don Philip Rinaldi, writing of this heavenly message of serene and captivating gentleness, refers to the patron of the order: "It is necessary that we have recourse to the Sacred Heart of Jesus to draw inspiration for the spirit of Saint Francis de Sales and Don Bosco; namely, for the meekness, the charity and the zeal in educating young people who were confided to Don Bosco in his first dream, and so to all of us who are carrying out his mission." (ASC Dec. 24, 1924)[8]

In a sense, then, the Congregation of Saint Francis de Sales was already prefigured in that dream of John Bosco when he was nine years of age. There was the promise of the Salesian heritage: a practical way of life combining reason, religion and loving kindness.

The "Meeting" with Saint Francis de Sales in the Seminary at Chieri (1835-1841)

As far as we know, the first spiritual contact that Don Bosco had with Saint Francis de Sales was during the period of his ecclesiastical formation at Chieri, through reading and study, religious instructions and conferences. In the seminary, Don Bosco's spirit of joy and his capacity for understanding others were characterized by a Salesian loving-kindness. (cf. S 67) The ideal of meekness of heart and gentleness in dealing with others had a great influence on the young cleric; these qualities stand out in the life of Saint Francis de Sales. Don Bosco's reading and meditating upon the example of the ardent apostle of the Chablais certainly helped form his image of the ideal priest.

One day there was a question about how John Bosco could be distinguished from a fellow seminarian with the same surname. Father Giacomelli relates:

John was called Bosco of Castelnuovo to distinguish him from another seminarian by the same surname, who later became director of the Rosine Institute in Turin. In this connection I remember a little incident which, though unimportant, impressed me. The two Boscos were joking about their names and wondering whether they should use some nickname for clarity's sake. The other Bosco said, "Bosco means wood. I like nespolo wood [which is hard and knotty], so call me Nespolo." [John replied,] "I instead like sales wood [Piedmontese for willow], which is soft and flexible, so call me Sales."

Was he perhaps already thinking about the future Society of Saint Francis de Sales while he tried to imitate the benignity of this saint? Sensitive as he was even in minor things, he would easily have been carried away by anger if he had been less virtuous. No other seminarian (and there were many) was so prone to flare up. It was evident, nevertheless, that John fought earnestly and steadily to keep his temper under control. (BM I, 302)

Don Bosco's Resolution at the Time of His Priestly Ordination (1841)

Throughout his seminary training, the cleric Bosco showed great promise and was so adjudged by his superiors. To be a good priest, however, enthusiasm and good resolutions were not enough. The seminarian had to be humble enough to seek direction, and Bosco did just that. To correctly discern his frequent dreams, such guidance was necessary.

He found an excellent guide in Father Cafasso, a priest totally dedicated to the service of souls, a man of deep piety and outstanding in meekness—truly a man of God. He was to be Don Bosco's "guardian angel" for over twenty years.

Because of this secure and providential guidance, Don Bosco was very well prepared for his longed-for goal, the priesthood; it was something he had dreamed of since his youth, despite the thousand-and-one difficulties which he had to overcome. He always had an image of the priesthood in his mind, but now he saw it in a new light. His only ambition was to be a priest totally consecrated to the spiritual good of young people. The resolutions he took on the occasion of his first Mass are a proof of his earnest resolve to live up to this holy and disinterested ideal.

He formulated his program in ten points, a decalogue, as it were, to be observed in his ministry. Among these resolutions, the ones relating to his special apostolate stand out; that is, the spiritual good of his friends, those young people he had seen in his dreams and whom he would certainly meet in the not-too-distant future. The fourth resolution is particularly significant: "The charity and gentleness of Saint Francis de Sales are to be my guide." (BM I, 385)

The careful choice of a patron saint was evident even at this stage. A whole gamut of possibilities lay before him. He could have been attracted by the zeal of a Saint Charles Borromeo, by the purity of a Saint Aloysius Gonzaga, above all by the cheerful spirit of a Saint Philip Neri. They were all well-known and beloved saints, invoked by so many. However, for his ministry among the young—he is still six months away from the beginning of this work—it is precisely charity, in the form of loving-kindness, which must be the distinguishing mark of his priesthood. Only by practicing this virtue would he succeed in his apostolate.

To be docile in cooperating with grace, to be gentle with the gentleness of Saint Francis de Sales—this he would try to be for the rest of his life.

> The resolutions taken by Don Bosco were certainly not motivated by weakness. They called for strength, as all who know his life fully realize. They demanded a tenacity of will which would allow no obstacles to stand in his way. By a close imitatation of his model, the young priest succeeded in mastering himself, to be calm when facing injustice, to preserve a constant good humor, to practice goodness with a firm constancy. (L'Arco, Don. *Il piu cortese dei santi*; P 44)

Patron and Personal Model

In view of the pressing needs of the apostolate, Don Bosco did not lose any time. Guided by the Blessed Virgin, who was to be the inspiration of all his enterprises, he sought to live out a conscientious program of learning to cultivate the virtue of meekness, so necessary in the exercise of charity toward those young people who needed his support. More than this, he methodically disciplined himself in order to moderate his lively and impulsive nature. Don Barberis testified to this: "His temperament tended to make him hotheaded, but he gained perfect control of himself. I can guarantee that I had never seen him lose his temper. I always admired in him a meekness and a gentleness comparable to that of his patron and ours." (P 45)

It is noteworthy that, according to the biographies of Saint Francis de Sales, the saint struggled for over twenty years to control his fiery character and become a model worthy of imitation. Don Bosco made a concerted effort to copy the bishop of Geneva in this regard. Those who lived with him in those early, heroic days at the oratory knew this. A passage in the *Biographical Memoirs* states: "He had studied in depth the life and works of this admirable apostle [Saint Francis de Sales], and when talking to his boys then, and later on as well, he would bring out some sayings or episodes of the saint's life. Above all he endeavored to portray to them the saint's gentleness, which had brought back to the Church so many heretics." (BM II, 197)

Don Bosco imitated Saint Francis de Sales throughout his whole life, putting himself under his protection, walking in his footsteps and emulating the actions of his model and patron.

He began his work and continued it under the guidance of the Blessed Virgin Mary. On the feast of the Immaculate Conception, December 8, 1841, Don Bosco received a poor, neglected orphan with kind words and friendly gestures. The charity and gentleness of Saint Francis de Sales guided and inspired him from the very beginning. Many others were to follow this lad, and in the course of time the Lord blessed Don Bosco's work with an increase that few could ever have imagined. (cf. MO 127)

Don Bosco's work did not have an easy or unimpeded birth; even his friends sometimes made things more difficult for him. However, the young priest had prepared himself for hardship by laying down the foundations of solid virtue which would allow him to stand alone. Besides gentleness, he needed courage; fortunately, as a boy and a young man he had begun to learn both. Following the heavenly advice of his first dream, he sought to become strong and stout-hearted, relying on the help which had been promised from on high.

In this effort he turned to Saint Francis de Sales for inspiration and protection, confiding in him as the patron of the work he was called upon to undertake. He had chosen Francis as his model of gentleness and charity, but he also recognized his great zeal for souls in his famous mission in the Chablais. In writing about Saint Vincent de Paul, Don Bosco linked the characteristics of both saints:

> Particularly in dealing with heretics, gentleness is very necessary. Saint Vincent de Paul used to say that the person with whom you are arguing is convinced that he is right. His aim is to win the argument at all costs, concerned not about recognizing the truth but in refuting it. If you try to argue with the same frame of mind, you will only succeed in shutting the door of his heart, while gentleness and affability keep that door open. The example of Saint Francis de Sales is an outstanding proof of this approach. The bishop of Geneva, although a brilliant debater, converted more heretics by his gentleness than by his learning. In this regard Cardinal Du Perron used to say that he realized he could win a debate with a Protestant but only Francis could convert him. I have never seen anyone converted except by a gentle approach. This is the only way to win souls for God. (LAS III, 301-302)

Don Bosco used this method himself, as witnessed by Canon Anfossi: "I myself was often present at Don Bosco's disputes with the Waldensians and greatly admired the subtle arguments Don Bosco employed. Obviously he must have prepared himself for the task, but he must also have had some supernatural assistance. This was particularly evidenced by the great charity with which he invariably treated these misguided people who were not always courteous to him. Don Bosco regarded kindness as the most indispensable virtue in dealing with heretics." (BM IV, 241)

5

Saint Francis de Sales, Patron of Don Bosco's Works

The First Oratory Named After Saint Francis de Sales (1844)

Neither the Oratory of Saint Francis de Sales nor the Salesian Congregation was a sudden brain-child of Don Bosco;

both had a slow and laborious birth. We will try to describe in a few words how difficult was the work of preparation and the consequent fatigue which Don Bosco had to bear before he was able to make his project on behalf of the young a reality.

Notwithstanding the trials and difficulties which he met at every turn and at every level, Don Bosco firmly believed that he should go ahead, entrusting himself in a special way to his holy patron. In the light of the teachings of the saint and imitating his example, as well as following the advice of Don Cafasso, he decided to get down to work immediately and so to lay the foundations of what was to become a grand enterprise.

The Lord's work generally has humble beginnings; it has the dimensions of the mustard seed in the Gospels. So Don Bosco was first satisfied with restricted quarters for his urchins—anything to have a roof over their heads. Part of his first humble dwelling was transformed into a chapel and dedicated to his holy protector. This was in the quarters conceded to him by the marchioness of Barolo, foundress of the *Refugio* in the Valdocco section of Turin. In a certain sense, things could not have gone better for Don Bosco, destitute as he was. By good fortune he made the acquaintance of the marchioness, his first benefactress, who was very generous. She too had a great devotion to Saint Francis de Sales. Among other good works, she was contemplating the foundation of a clerical religious institute which, bearing the name of her patron, would draw its inspiration from his doctrine and especially from his practice of the apostolic life. At the entrance to a new building destined for the chaplains, as if in preparation for this, she had hung a painting of the saint, which she had commissioned. Don Bosco, as a young priest, would have passed by this painting frequently during his stay at the institute as a chaplain.

Stella remarks:

Just happening upon such a picture might well have seemed providential to him, however, since that choice of patron certainly suited his own inner aspirations, which he yearned to make manifest and justify. In the oldest regulations for the oratory known to us (to be dated 1851-1852), we read that the oratory is placed "under the protection of Saint Francis de

Sales, because those who intend to dedicate themselves to this kind of work should adopt this saint as their model of charity and affability, the latter being the wellsprings of the fruit we expect to derive from the work of the oratories." (S 108)

Later, in his *Memoirs of the Oratory*, Don Bosco offered several reasons why he chose Saint Francis de Sales as his patron:

1. Because the marchioness Barolo had the intention of founding a congregation of priests under that title, and with that in mind had had the saint's picture painted at the entranceway, where it can still be found.

2. Because our kind of ministry called for great calm and gentleness, and so we placed ourselves under the protection of this saint so that he might obtain for us from God the grace to imitate his extraordinary gentleness and his winning of souls. Another reason . . . was that he might help us from heaven to imitate him in combatting errors against religion, especially Protestantism, which was beginning to insinuate itself into our localities, and noticeably into the city of Turin. (MO 141; cf. BM II, 196-197)

A long-awaited chapel was blessed in 1844; even though it was used for only a short time, it was an important milestone in a work which was to become permanent. With the first chapel in honor of Don Bosco's holy patron, the oratory assumed its name and had its real beginning. It was called "The Oratory of Saint Francis de Sales." Stella notes:

In 1844 Don Bosco transferred to the Refuge and the little hospital or infirmary (*Ospedaletto*) of Marchioness Barolo, serving as an assistant to Father Borel. He was followed there by the group of youths who had gathered around him at the *Convitto*, and he did not send them away. Then and there he started the oratory, which he named after Saint Francis de Sales. If he did that with all due consideration, then it was one of the most carefully calculated and decisive steps he had ever taken in his life so far. (ibid., 107)

This happy coincidence—the erection of a chapel and the naming of an incipient work—is pregnant with meaning. Don Bosco, we believe, understood this and appreciated its historical importance. In the first place he wanted to pay tribute to his great benefactor, the marchioness Barolo, and this he did by setting up an oratory at her hospice and dedicating it to a saint who was very dear to her. This may be described as a casual motive, but another, more convincing one, bears greater weight. The oratory, uncertain in its beginnings, would have a more solid foundation if placed under the protection of a saint who was well-known and whose characteristic virtues made him an outstanding model of charity toward the young. The virtues of kindness and constancy were the hallmarks of this great apostle and missionary, and these were the very virtues that work in the oratory required. Moreover, only in this way could heresy, which was threatening the city of Turin at the time, be combatted and neutralized. This is how a new apostolate came into being under the protection of the apostle of the Chablais. Lemoyne wrote:

> While still at the *Convitto*, Don Bosco had inwardly decided to place all his undertakings under the protection of the apostle of the Chablais, but before disclosing this intention of his he waited for Father Cafasso to express his opinion on this point. And Father Cafasso did so. One day, talking with Father Borel about Don Bosco's difficulties, his patience in all his dealings, and the continuous growth of the oratory, Father Cafasso remarked that, until then, this work had not been placed under the protection of a patron saint. After a brief discussion, he suggested Saint Francis de Sales, and Father Borel agreed. (cf. BM II, 196)

Meanwhile the number of youngsters who were following Don Bosco kept growing. They could be counted in the hundreds and desperately needed more space. The future oratory was just a dream in Don Bosco's mind, but he was working and planning to make it a reality as soon as possible. Some thought that he was on the verge of a nervous breakdown. Yet there were those who supported him through thick and thin—people who trusted him in their hearts, even if they could not understand his visionary plans. Such a one was Don Cafasso. With him Don Bosco discussed all the dreams that eventually came true: the purchase of the Pinardi shed and property, the building of the Church of Saint Francis de Sales, the acquiring of additional land for future expansion, the establishment of a printshop and other workshops, and the publication of the *Catholic Readings*. Sometimes, while conversing with the boys, Don Bosco would unwittingly give a hint of these new plans; at the time they sounded like daydreams, but they were all to come true. It could not have been otherwise, because they were God-inspired. (cf. BM IV, 410)

Although the oratory had not yet found a permanent home in 1844, it had its chapel, a very modest one indeed, under the singular title of the saintly Savoyard.

The Pinardi Shed and the First Church in Honor of Saint Francis de Sales (1846-1852)

Barely two years had passed since the dedication of the first chapel in the Barolo Institute. On April 12, 1846, in a new home, Don Bosco had the joy of witnessing the blessing of the newly-acquired Pinardi shed, adapted as a chapel and dedicated to Saint Francis de Sales. As a memento and a sign of his devotion, he hung up a small picture of the saint. Another step was taken in the founding of the oratory. (cf. P 54)

Things moved quickly and, we must admit, not always in favor of the poor priest from Valdocco. All the same, Don Bosco, with untiring zeal and with the help of generous benefactors, succeeded in building a real church. This was the first structure he had built himself; the others he had adapted or simply repaired. All this was done, not merely by human means, but with supernatural support. We can see a continuity and progression: at the Barolo Institute, a small room (1844); then a new site at Valdocco—the Pinardi shed; a chapel (1846) and finally a church (1852). (cf. P 55; BM IV, Ch. 38)

In a letter to Rosmini on May 28, 1851 (E I, 45), Don Bosco wrote with a certain sense of satisfaction that this was the first church in Piedmont built for the use of abandoned youth.

Don Bosco was very attached to the Church of Saint Francis de Sales. It was first planned in his mind and then built with his heart. For this reason it has rightly been claimed by his early helpers as the cradle of his work and of the congregation itself. One of Don Bosco's first biographers comments: "The true Salesian Portiuncula is and always will be the Church of Saint Francis de Sales, full of so many memories." (Amadei I, 257; P 55)

Don Bosco was confident of this all along. One day, wishing to dispel Father Borel's anxiety and assure him of his own perfect sanity, he confided to him in strict secrecy how God and the Blessed Virgin had shown him in a vision that the Valdocco area would be the birthplace of the Oratory of Saint Francis de Sales and of the religious congregation which he intended to found.

This revelation filled Father Borel with joy. He never forgot it and often repeated these words of Don Bosco. In 1857, when he saw the first part of the present Oratory of Saint Francis de Sales, he remarked to Michael Rua, then a cleric: "In his predictions, Don Bosco described this house to me exactly as it stands now. I have to admit that what he said about having seen those buildings in his dreams has now been fully realized." (BM II, 326)

On this topic there is no better source than Father Giraudi, the most notable commentator on the whole project and its development. He was economer-general for many years and wrote a masterpiece on the oratory.

> The Church of Saint Francis de Sales . . . was the first building constructed by Don Bosco, and for sixteen years, from June 1852 to June 1868, was the place which witnessed the piety, the Eucharistic fervor and all the religious life of hundreds and thousands of youngsters formed at his school . . . In this Church of Saint Francis de Sales, Mamma Margaret had observed Savio intent on his practices of piety and in fervent prayer even after the formal prayers were over . . . In it were also formed the first illustrious sons of Don Bosco . . . It was the center in which Don Bosco exercised the ministry of the confessional and preaching . . . For four years Mamma Margaret prayed in this chapel frequently during the day . . . Just outside the side door, Don Bosco, in November 1860, worked the miracle of the multiplication of the bread which he handed out to over four hundred boys, although the basket contained only about twenty buns. This church, converted into a mortuary chapel, received the venerated remains of Don Bosco in 1888 and Don Rua in 1910, before whose bodies an immense crowd of people filed for several days . . . (Giraudi 117-119)

A Foreshadowing of Future Projects (1850)

At the same time as the idea of building a church in honor of Saint Francis de Sales was in Don Bosco's mind, he was also thinking of constructing "a temple not made by man." He envisioned a group of people who would live the Gospel and give witness to it by good works. It was the Salesian ideal of a combination of the active and the contemplative life, for people who lived in the world and wanted to unite the roles of Martha and Mary. They would give of themselves with a very deep spirit of abnegation and charity on behalf of the poor, nourished by the liturgy of praise and self-offering. Because of the political situation, however, they would have to work almost secretly, without attracting attention.

This was a novel idea at that period in the history of the Church, or rather a return to a way of life formulated and lived by the saints—such men as Saint Philip Neri and Saint Vincent de Paul—at the time of the Counter-Reformation. The choice of a patron or titular was very important for such a daring apostolate. It was not by mere chance that Don Bosco put the work under the protection of Saint Francis de Sales. Under the saint's patronage, his works and plans gradually evolved. (P 57)

We focus our attention for the moment on a special period in the life of the saint and on the establishment of a work which, although only in its embryonic stage, foreshadowed the future Union of Salesian Cooperators. For this reason alone the period deserves to be better known and so given a rightful place in all its historical-ascetical dimensions.

At the end of the year 1850, Don Bosco accepted an invitation to give a mission in the Church of Saint Sempliciano in Milan. Here he made some very useful contacts with people involved in various works on behalf of the young in the Lombard capital. He began to design a plan:

> What God wanted of him had always been clear in his mind ever since he had started his oratories. Even at that time he had given much thought to the help that Catholic laymen could give to the bishops and priests, provided that they were trained to participate in the defense of a Christian society. Many were not to grasp the significance of this concept until later. He also realized the importance of an association which would unite his benefactors in the pursuit of his aims. He was then toying with the idea of starting, on a small scale and cautiously, an association whose members later were to be known as "Salesian Cooperators." (BM IV, 120)

A formal statement of purpose was set out in seven articles under the date of November 17, 1850. It documented the erection of an association with the aim of defending the Catholic religion against current errors. This embryonic gathering of lay people bore the name of a pious union under the protection of Saint Francis de Sales. The reason for this choice was clearly stated in Article 1: "To form a provisional pious union under the patronage of Saint Francis de Sales. This saint has been chosen because of the similarity between present conditions in our country and those in Savoy during his times." (ibid.)

As to the name, there were many suggestions; it changed from being called a society, a consortium, an association. However, it was a genuinely lay institution, as Don Bosco's biographer did not hesitate to call it. What is even more important is the fact that a very precise and extensive program was outlined.

First of all there was a proposal to fight against evil; better—whenever that was possible—to prevent it. Every initiative would require episcopal approval and the support of the clergy, especially the parish priests. It was the intent of the movement to broaden the base of apostolic action by giving truly Christian witness, with due regard for prudence. According to their natural talent and the nature of the work, the members were to be organized into three distinct groups.

For whatever reason, this lay organization never got off the ground; we hear no more about it in the whole history of the oratory. Nevertheless, this aborted union certainly laid the foundation for what would eventually become the Union of Salesian Cooperators. The labor involved in this enterprise, undertaken in imitation of the apostolic and missionary efforts of Saint Francis de Sales, would bear fruit in its own time.

We should not forget that the ecclesiastical authority of Turin admired Don Bosco's apostolate, especially the oratories. Archbishop Fransoni never failed to support him and urged him to carry on with the task he had undertaken, which he considered his own. In an official letter dated March 31, 1852, he effectively appointed Don Bosco "the director and spiritual head of the Oratory of Saint Francis de Sales." (cf. P 59; Annali I, 11)

So this incipient institution had the blessing of the Church, a full and benevolent approbation of the whole undertaking and, as far as the lifestyle and activities were concerned, ample faculties to work and expand into new ventures. All of this was under the amiable protection of the holy bishop of Geneva.

The Apostolate of the Press and the *Salesian Bulletin* (1852-1877)

As the years progressed, the figure of the holy protector was clearly kept in focus. This was true also in regard to the apostolate of the press, for the name Salesian came to be associated with this form of Catholic action. Don Bosco did not rest as long as there was need of finding new ways and means to accomplish the momumental work of evangelization. Here again the saint was ahead of his times, truly a man of prophetic and long-range vision. He was convinced that one of the most efficacious means of spreading and defending Catholic truth was by means of the Catholic press. (cf. Annali I, 685-687; *Salesian Bulletin*, April 1882)

In the course of time, Don Bosco was able to produce and distribute good books and other written materials as an excellent antidote against error and heresy. Here too he was treading in the footsteps of his patron. He had the courage of his convictions and wanted to imitate the Doctor of Charity in defending Catholic truth. Don Bosco put his whole heart and soul into this apostolate, multiplying books and pamphlets for the young. The circulation of his *Catholic Readings* kept growing. In the brevity of its articles and its lively style, it was very much after the pattern of the leaflets distributed centuries before by Saint Francis de Sales in the Chablais. Don Bosco understood and admired the saint, long before the importance of the Catholic press was recognized and before Saint Francis de Sales was proclaimed the patron of journalists. In a letter written years later (March 1885), he explicitly stated his support of writings permeated with the spirit of the saint:

The apostolate of good books is one of the principal aims of our congregation . . . I am particularly interested in the sector of youth. I have always tried to help young people, not only by the spoken word but by the printed word as well. With the *Catholic Readings* . . . , with the *"Giovane Provveduto,"* with the *History of Italy* (and with other works), I wanted to assist young people in their studies and to protect them from the many errors that would be dangerous for their temporal and eternal welfare . . . Finally, with the *Salesian Bulletin*, together with its other aims, there was this one: to keep alive in the hearts of the young the love of the spirit of Saint Francis de Sales and his maxims, and so form them to be apostles of other young people . . . I beg and beseech you . . . by your words and by your example to help me to form young people to be *so many apostles in the spreading of good books.* (E IV, 320-321)

Here we clearly see Don Bosco's ideal of making all his past pupils collaborators—Salesians, as it were—in the world. "By the name of Salesians I really mean all those who were educated in the spirit of the teaching of the great saint [Saint Francis de Sales]. So, for all intents and purposes, you are all Salesians." (MB XVII, 176-177)

In our own day we have come to realize how far Don Bosco was ahead of his times in his efforts to implement the principles of the apostolate in the spirit of Saint Francis de Sales. He faced up to the challenges, like his patron, with serenity and decisiveness. As a result, his collaborators were convinced that, in following Saint Francis de Sales as their master and teacher, they were inheritors with Don Bosco of a living tradition inspired by the Holy Spirit.

To profit as much as possible by the use of the press, Don Bosco intended that the *Salesian Bulletin* would be the official instrument to spread the ideas and the work of his congregation; i.e., a vehicle for the promulgation of the spirit of Saint Francis de Sales. The *Salesian Bulletin* made its appearance in August 1877. In a very decisive way, Don Bosco called for the assistance of the Salesian Cooperators, in the name of Francis de Sales and with a totally apostolic and ecclesial goal. Beginning in February 1878 (with No. 6), the front page of the monthly magazine featured a picture of the holy patron.

One of the most notable quotations, a characteristic Salesian expression, went like this: "A tender love toward one's neighbor is one of the greatest and most excellent gifts which divine goodness could bestow on men." This was almost to proclaim the watchword as well as the style or approach. In the first issues and for a good period of time, maxims of Saint Francis de Sales and episodes from his life were reprinted. This was particularly true as the liturgical feast of January 29 drew near, and for the external celebration of the feast on the following Sunday. The customary insignia of every issue was the picture of Saint Francis de Sales.

6
Saint Francis de Sales, Patron of Don Bosco's Followers

The First Promoters or Collaborators (1845-1852)

We have seen how Don Bosco had thought of establishing a group of people who would support him in his work for young people in the oratories. Above all, he needed help from the laity. He wrote an initial draft for such a group as far back as 1841. (cf. BM XI, 60) His original plan never materialized as he had envisioned it; yet he had lay collaborators whom he formed into an association with no juridical status. In 1847 he wrote for them a simple set of regulations to be observed according to each one's possibilities. (cf. BM III, 67) This group of lay persons formed the Congregation of Saint Francis de Sales before the clerical Society of Saint Francis de Sales came into existence. The *Biographical Memoirs* tells of its origin and history:

> . . . A few laymen joined together to perform the many varied tasks [connected with these boys], and they contributed to the support of the so-called festive oratories, either by their personal services or with donations. They were known by the name of the office they held, but as a rule they were called benefac-

tors, promoters, and also Cooperators of the Congregation of Saint Francis de Sales . . . The so-called Salesian promotors and cooperators, banded together in a regular congregation known as the Congregation of Saint Francis de Sales, first received a few spiritual favors from the Holy See in a rescript dated April 18, 1845 . . . In 1850 Don Bosco informed His Holiness that a congregation had been legitimately established in the city of Turin in the name and under the protection of Saint Francis de Sales, and implored more extensive favors on behalf of its members, besides other spiritual benefits for the nonmembers. These favors were granted in a rescript dated September 28, 1850 . . . (BM XI, 73-74)

Don Bosco clearly indicated Saint Francis de Sales as the patron of this initial group dedicated to the advancement and salvation of young people. The founder presented him once more as an outstanding model of ascetical practice and spirituality. In doing so he stressed his simple approach and his great success in winning souls. "The only aim of the Oratory of Saint Francis de Sales is to save souls. This oratory is placed under the patronage of Saint Francis de Sales, because those who intend to dedicate themselves to this kind of work should adopt this saint as a model of charity and affability. These sources will produce the fruits that we expect from the oratories." (BM III, 68)

Don Bosco's biographer, speaking as if stating a well-known fact, clearly states: ". . . Don Bosco believed that the spirit of Saint Francis de Sales was the best suited, at the time, for the education and upbringing of the working classes." (BM II, 197)

Don Bosco was convinced that help from the laity was necessary for his specific apostolate among young people. This is why he wanted to form them into a congregation. As time went on and circumstances changed, he came to realize that a mere set of regulations for his lay helpers would not ensure the continuance of his work. He would also need a group of religious approved by the Church in order to realize his dream. From then on, Don Bosco began to pin his hopes on the promising young men for whom and with whom he was working. In the boys of the oratory, in particular, he saw his greatest prospects. All the same, these first collaborators merit our attention for the great good they managed to do.

It is worth noting that all those promotors to whom the adjective Salesian was first given and applied by Don Bosco were members of the laity. This is, in itself, a very interesting innovation. In time there was to be a set of regulations drawn up for their guidance: "The rules had their beginning, Don Bosco tells us, when, as the number of Cooperators increased, they themselves unanimously requested some sort of regulations which would help them to retain uniformity of spirit . . . and assure stability to their organization." (BM XI, 76)

These regulations were formulated and given a specific name only about 1876.

In the light of subsequent changes and transformations, this first stage is of paramount importance. These energies were not wasted; they foreshadowed future events. The existence and vitality of the early helpers prefigured a society which would withstand the test of time.

The First Salesians Are Born (1854)

In successive reports forwarded to the Holy See, reference was continually made to the evolution of the initial association into the Society of Saint Francis de Sales. Don Bosco described this development in the explanation he gave to the archbishop of Turin in 1876:

> In 1858 the Congregation (of Cooperators) was divided into two sections or rather into two families:
>
> • Those who were free of family ties and felt they had a vocation to stay that way, joined together in common life. They lived in the house that had always been the motherhouse and center of that pious association which the supreme pontiff suggested be called the Pious Society of Saint Francis de Sales. It is still called by that name.
>
> • The others, or the day students, continued to live in the world and in the bosoms of their families, but they also continued to promote the work of the oratories, retaining to this day the name of Union or Congregation of Saint Francis de Sales, of Promotors or Cooperators—but always in dependence on the professed members with whom they unite to work for the sake of poor youth. (Aubry II, 77; cf. BM XI, 74)

Don Ceria makes a similar point in the *Annali*:

> That providence had been preparing Don Bosco for a long time to be the creator and organizer of the large religious family

called that of Saint Francis de Sales is a fact which cannot be doubted. His life, guided as by an invisible hand, seems to us today to have been preordained for the execution of a plan which God had kept secret within his own counsel; besides, the successive events in his life were intermingled with not infrequent manifestations full of mystery and prophecy whereby Don Bosco would be chosen as the instrument for God's glory and the good of souls, in times which were so perilous for the Church. (Annali I, 3-4)

As time went on, Don Bosco's thoughts were centered more and more on the oratory itself, and particularly on those persons in the oratory who showed the most promise. He did not hesitate to share his ideals with these young people in a simple way, after the manner of the bishop of Geneva. The Oratory of Saint Francis de Sales became a fruitful source from which seeds could sprout and grow.

Shortly after the construction of the Church of Saint Francis de Sales in 1852, there was an edifice of another kind, "built upon living stones." (cf. 1 Pt 2:5) Don Bosco was able to get considerable economic help from his benefactors. He was convinced, however, that he also needed to organize a group of trustworthy disciples who would continue his work. We read in the *Biographical Memoirs*:

As the feast of Saint Francis de Sales was approaching, Don Bosco again tried in a roundabout way to instill the idea of a religious congregation in the minds of a few of his pupils. He summoned them to a meeting, during which he spoke about the good that many of them could do for their fellow men in general and boys in particular if they were all united into one body. Preserved in our archives are the minutes of this meeting as recorded by the cleric Rua, from which we learn the following:

On the evening of January 26, 1854, we gathered in Don Bosco's room. Present were Don Bosco, [Joseph] Rocchietti, Artiglia, [John] Cagliero and [Michael] Rua. Don Bosco suggested that, with the help of the Lord and Saint Francis de Sales, we should first test ourselves by performing deeds of charity toward our neighbor, then bind ourselves by a promise, and later, if possible and desirable, make a formal vow to God. From that evening on, those who agreed—or would later agree—to this were called "Salesians." (BM V, 8)

It is well to pause here to make an observation and to have a deeper look at what is understood by this name of Salesians. In the first place, the time chosen was most opportune, as it was during the period of intense preparation for the saint's feast day. So it could be said that this was a form of devotion and consecration for the big day. The figure of the patron, highlighted by appropriate readings of his works and episodes from his life, particularly his wonderful example of zeal and gentleness in the exercise of charity, would have been a grand incentive for these young lads to throw themselves into this new and binding kind of apostolate.

While the name of Salesians is auspicious, ways were sought to guarantee its fruitfulness. De Sales was invoked as the protector, and his qualities or specific virtues were kept well in mind. These lads who bore his name could not help but be inspired by the milieu in which they lived. Don Bosco himself seemed to them to be a living image of the patron. They were well aware, as Father Ceria records, that the oratory got its name from Saint Francis de Sales, that the church built two years before was dedicated to him, and that Don Bosco had a very strong devotion to this saint. (cf. Annali I, 15)

The Society of Saint Francis de Sales

Although this initial group of Salesians became more numerous as time went on, no society as such existed; better, it existed *de facto* but not *de jure*. The consent and approval of Church authority and of the proper Roman congregations was needed. The name of the Salesian Congregation or Society—in a true and proper sense—first made its appearance in an official form in the drafting of the *Constitutions* which date back to 1858. In a famous audience—the first—which Pope Pius IX granted Don Bosco on March 21 of that year, the name was used in the presentation of the history of Don Bosco's work.

Alongside the official date of January 26, 1854, we should place another one, equally prophetic—that of December 18, 1859. On that day, with the first consecration and taking of vows, to all intents and purposes the society became a formal entity. Shortly before that date, Don Bosco explained to the Salesians who had gathered in his room that it was now time to establish the congregation formally and to accept the rules. He allowed them ten days to think it over. On the evening of December 18, at the meeting at which one's acceptance was to be declared, only two failed to present themselves. The following is an extract from the historical document which constituted the act of foundation. The participants met

> . . . in Don Bosco's room at nine o'clock in the evening . . . decided to band themselves together into a society or congregation which, while aiming at the sanctification of each member by mutual assistance, would strive to promote God's glory and the salvation of souls, especially of those in greater need of instruction and formation. After unanimous endorsement of these goals and after a short prayer and invocation of the Holy Spirit, the participants proceeded to the election of officers of the said society . . . (BM VI, 181-182)

That must have been a moment of deep emotion for Don Bosco—one of great trepidation but also of great joy. In all truth he could say that the new society was his creation. It had been the object of his full attention for quite a long time. He had procured a solid foundation for his congregation and provided for its structures and continuity. He could be confident of a high degree of protection from above, because all would be placed under the patronage of our Lady and of Saint Francis de Sales. It was from the titular that the motivating drive and inspiration flowed, to provide guidelines and ensure the future growth of the society. The saint's presence was honored, his intercession invoked and his powerful protection daily felt. He was, so to speak, always at Don Bosco's side, always in his thoughts and sometimes even in his dreams.

The resolution adopted by Don Bosco at the time of his first Mass, of trying to become a faithful spiritual son of Saint Francis de Sales, was passed on to all his Salesians.

The Daughters of Mary Help of Christians
(Salesian Sisters)

A number of years after the establishment of the Society of Saint Francis de Sales, Don Bosco founded a religious congregation of women, the Institute of the Daughters of Mary Help of Christians (FMA), popularly known as the Salesian

Sisters. It would be beyond the scope of the present work to go into detail about the origins of this foundation, but we will briefly sketch its history.

Don Bosco arranged that the election of a superior and chapter should take place on the feast of Saint Francis de Sales in 1872. The co-foundress, Mother Mary Mazzarello, was elected the first superior. She was deeply devoted to Don Bosco, enamored of his spirit and very receptive to the direction he gave either in person or through the spiritual directors he sent. He frequently invoked the moderation of Francis de Sales to temper the sisters' early tendency to be extreme in penance and prolonged prayer—due partly to the inexperience and overzealousness of one of the directors.

Little things, hidden things done well and with love, interior more than exterior penances, sacrifice of the will, short but devout prayer, work and walks in the orchard, serenity and joy at all times—such were Don Bosco's recommendations.

The Mornese Sisters put up a sign reading, significantly: "This is the house of the love of God." A saying popular among the pioneer FMA's "never to give offense, never to take offense"—in reference to community life—came from Francis de Sales's correspondence. Don Bosco's first letter to Mornese, "Keep up your prayers, but throw yourselves heart and soul into your work," could have been postmarked Geneva.

Once when Don Bosco was visiting the Daughters of Mary Help of Christians, he left them four important counsels: awareness of God's presence; love of work; practice of kindliness and joy; and zeal for the salvation of souls.[9] These are certainly key features of the Salesian spirit and are easily discovered in the writings of Saint Francis de Sales, although Don Bosco may not have intended to attribute them to his patron at the time of his recommendation to the sisters.

In the *Introduction to the Devout Life*, Saint Francis de Sales wrote that work, as well as fasting, serves as penance, provided the labor undertaken contributes to the glory of God and one's own welfare. He preferred the pain of labor to physical suffering. Various sayings of Saint Francis give us an idea of his spirituality:

Youth and idleness are bad companions; the latter betrays the former. Have always in hand some good work, either corporal or spiritual . . . We are all fishers, and fishers of men, and so should we in our fishing not only employ care, labor and night hours, but make use of every allurement, every tactic, every bait; yea, even, if I may be so bold as to say it, every kind of holy diplomacy . . . Never harbor the temptation to sadness. It is the enemy of all devotion. Why should there be sadness in a servant of Him who will be our joy forever? . . . Most of the faults committed by good people arise from their not sufficiently keeping a steadfast recollection of the presence of God . . . Those who love God cannot cease to think of Him, aspire after Him, speak of Him, live for Him . . . Do not think that our Lord is far from you while you are in the midst of the bustle and pressure of affairs called for by your vocation . . . What most attracts Him is the welcome we give to the accomplishment in us of His holy will and of our will in Him . . . I recommend to you above all the spirit of gentleness.[10]

The Association of Salesian Cooperators

From the beginning of his work, Don Bosco was helped by lay promoters or collaborators, who eventually became known as Salesian Cooperators—the third branch of the Salesian family. There was an evolution in his mind and in the actual unfolding of events. He had the idea of lay helpers right at the start of his work with young people, as we have already pointed out, but the Cooperators as a distinct organization received official sanction by the Holy See only in 1876.

Don Bosco intended the Cooperators to be "extern Salesians," but he encountered many difficulties in trying to get this form of apostolic dedication approved. In practical terms the association was similar to a third order, common to various congregations and institutes—a kind of Christian union of people coming together with the principal aim of doing good works, especially on behalf of abandoned youth. And yet Don Bosco wanted the Cooperators to become, not a mere band of helpers, but something better and greater. He envisioned them as Catholics active in the world, dedicated not only to their own sanctification but to the spread of everything good within their families and throughout society as a whole.

It is of interest to see with what spirit Don Bosco wanted these lay people animated. This can be easily discerned from the regulations composed by him, which stress that they must be the leaven of sanctification among the masses by means of the spirit of Saint Francis de Sales; namely, with a zeal animated by charity and gentle kindness, with a desire to save one's soul and one's neighbor's by prayer and action. These were the fundamental ideas emphasized by Don Bosco in a talk he gave to the Cooperators in 1883.

One hundred years later, hundreds of thousands of people have rallied to Don Bosco's call to be Salesian Cooperators. They and many others are served by the *Salesian Bulletin*, now published on every continent in thirty-nine editions and twelve languages, with a combined circulation of 1,083,000 copies.

Part I in Retrospect

We have traced the early historical connection between Saint John Bosco and Saint Francis de Sales. The following is a resumé of the "spiritual consanguinity" between them, drawn up by Rev. John Ayers, SDB.

From the Beginning

As early as 1720, there existed widespread Associations of Saint Francis de Sales, with thousands of members—lay and religious—from Savoy to Piedmont. Included among the members were Don Cafasso and the rector of the seminary at Chieri where Don Bosco was a student. Saint Francis de Sales had a close personal association with Turin and Chieri, where he frequently stayed. The historical connection of the saint with these areas made him known and remembered there.

At the Seminary

In the Chieri seminary, John Bosco was known as "Bosco di Sales" to distinguish him from another student of the same name, "Bosco di Nespoli." This was not merely a play on words, "flexible" as opposed to "inflexible," but was a tribute to Don Bosco's already-existing devotion to the gentle saint. This is confirmed by his pre-ordination resolution in which he pledged: "The charity and gentleness of Saint Francis de Sales are to be my guide." Earlier, as a seminarian, he had taken two of his patron's maxims as a guide: 1) "To accompany and not to anticipate the steps of divine providence—not one step ahead, not one step behind"; 2) "To ask for nothing; to refuse nothing."

At the Convitto

In both the seminary and the *Convitto* postgraduate house where Don Bosco studied, pictures of Saint Francis de Sales were venerated. The superior of the *Convitto* was widely known as "the living image of the bishop of Geneva." Before leaving this house of studies, Don Bosco took counsel of both Don Cafasso and Don Borel about the choice of patron for his blossoming youth work. Both advised Francis de Sales, confirming the decision he had already made in his own mind.

At the Rifugio

As chaplain to the hospital of Saint Philomena, where Marchioness Barolo had earlier planned to found her own congregation of Salesian priests, Don Bosco not only blessed a mural of the saint but opened a new chapel in his honor.

At the First Oratory and Chapel

Don Bosco dedicated his first oratory and Pinardi shed-chapel to Francis de Sales; his patron's portrait held pride of place behind the main altar. This chapel no longer stands in its original form, but it has been restored. Having outgrown the Pinardi chapel, Don Bosco erected his first church proper, once again dedicated to his patron.

The Regulations

The very first copy of the oratory regulations (1852) states that the oratory was placed under the patronage of Saint Francis de Sales because much patience and charity would be necessary to accomplish its mission.

The First Salesians

In 1854, on the first day of the triduum for the feast of Saint Francis de Sales, Don Bosco brought together the first group of clerics and gave them the name of Salesians . . . bound only by the bonds of brotherly love for the exercise of charity toward their neighbor, especially poor and abandoned youth. So reads Don Rua's journal. (cf. BM V, 7-8)

The Motto

From the testimony of Dominic Savio, we see that by 1856 his patron's motto, *Da mihi animas,* was already Don Bosco's own. Francis's image appeared as part of the emblem on the front cover of the first *Salesian Bulletin,* as it did on the title page of the first Salesian rule. On vigils of feast days, the illuminated initials O.S.F.S. (Oratory of Saint Francis de Sales) lighted up the oratory's skyline.

In Practice

Father John Bonetti gives us his testimony as a pioneer pupil. Don Bosco often told his boys how Francis de Sales acquired calmness and gentleness, not from natural temperament but by great sacrifice, self-control and prayer. They knew then that Don Bosco was unwittingly describing his own self-mastery to acquire the same kindness and patience as his patron. To both pupils and Salesians, Don Bosco often referred to Francis's ardent, apostolic zeal—in particular how he had endured both hostility and alpine cold to win 70,000 souls to the Church of Jesus Christ, becoming all things to all men. (cf. 1 Cor 9:22; see Bonetti, G. *Saint John Bosco's Early Apostolate.*)

PART II

Years of Maturity

A Spirit Emerges

7

Comparison Between the Two Saints

To their devotees, Francis de Sales and Don Bosco appear as saints extraordinarily adorned with gifts of nature and of grace, expressed both in the loftiness of their doctrine and in their practice of the most exalted virtues.

There are several points of similarity that can be dwelt on in detail: 1) their respective spiritualities; 2) the pastoral and educative motivation of their zeal; 3) the similar way they practiced some of the virtues. Looking at early Salesian tradition, we find that these important elements were faithfully handed down by Don Bosco's first successors.

Convergence in Ideals

In comparing Francis de Sales with Don Bosco, it is better to speak of a common spirit than a common spirituality as such. The latter is proper and clearly defined for each of them. Our task is to extract all that is essential in the doctrine of Saint Francis de Sales and see how Don Bosco made it his own and gave it, so to speak, a practical slant. Apart from the fundamental element, truly evangelical and common to both, which is love, there are three pivotal points: a devout and optimistic humanism; the universal call to holiness for everyone; and the ecstasy of life or union with God.

A Devout and Optimistic Humanism

That cultural and religious movement known as Christian humanism, which dominated and characterized the nineteenth century, was opposed to pagan humanism and the paganizing elements of the Renaissance. We can trace its specific intonations and dominant notes to the devout humanism of Saint Francis de Sales. His writings and talks display an aristocratic content and a healthy religiosity, which he used as the basis of "an intimate, strong and generous devotion." (O I, 13) This is seen very clearly in the saint's first work, *Introduction to the Devout Life*.

Francis de Sales wished to convince the ordinary person that true devotion is neither difficult to understand nor hard to practice. Religion can be adapted to any level of living, made suitable for any social condition and inserted into the routine occupations of daily life. We could call it a devotion adapted to day-to-day living. At the core of this teaching, human beings are exalted in all their dignity, turned toward God both in body and in spirit. A devout humanism, translated into practical terms and sustained by love, is attractive to the human heart, which is naturally inclined to love God ever more and more. He is the "God of the human heart." (O IV, 74)

The devout humanism of Saint Francis de Sales became in Don Bosco an optimistic humanism; one could qualify his devotion as human, serene and liberating. The apostle of new times addressed young people in a language adapted to them and understood by them—a spirit of joy which attracted them and conquered their hearts. Its dominant note is expressed in the words of the psalmist: ". . . serve the LORD with gladness." (Ps. 100:2)

Don Bosco gave of himself generously, smilingly, with an open and understanding heart. Deeply a man and a man of God, he did not close his eyes to human weakness, nor did he minimize it; yet he knew how to bring spiritual power into play for a valid and secure retention of all that is good, making use of every available resource hidden within the heart of a young person. As the *Salesian Constitutions* put it: "Inspired by the optimistic humanism of Saint Francis de Sales, the follower of Don Bosco relies on every human resource, natural and supernatural, without losing sight of human weakness." (Art. 17)

Quite rightly one can speak of an integral Salesian humanism. In 1972 the Salesian General Chapter seized this expression and spoke of an integral Christian promotion and a liberating Christian education. It is the same language as that used by Don Bosco, who loved to speak of a program of life that was proposed to the boys in simple but deep-meaning formulae. He wanted to mold good Christians and honest citizens, strove for good health, wisdom and sanctity in the formation of his boys, and put before them a way of life that could be summed up as "joy, study and piety." These words express the meaning of a devout and optimistic humanism which is typically Salesian. (*Twentieth General Chapter of the Salesians*, 81)

A Universal Call to Holiness

Another key element of Salesian spirituality, in perfect accord with the preceding one—even a logical consequence— is the fact that Saint Francis de Sales declared sanctity to be the call of grace for all Christians in the Church of the Lord. He had no hesitation in proposing the idea, as a fundamental component, that to seek God is natural to the human spirit.

The Church, according to the thought of the bishop of Geneva, does not limit itself to promoting the ideal of a devout life only to more lofty souls, but encourages and cultivates a profound aspiration, an authentic inclination for which all souls hunger: to be saints in Christ through the sanctifying power of the Spirit. (cf. Rom 1:4)

For Francis de Sales, humanism took on a concrete expression: it was expanded into a Christian humanism. From "devout" it became "Christocentric," since only in the God-man is there redemption, sanctification and salvation. However, besides the *Introduction*, Francis wrote the *Treatise on the Love of God*; that is to say, from a simple introduction to a devout life he went on to a complete treatise on the constant love of God. A program of devotion for all is transformed into a clear-cut ascetical and mystical declaration, expressing the ideal of perfectly adhering to the will of God.

The Doctor of Love clearly proclaimed: "If we want to become saints in our own way, we will never become saints. We must become saints as the Lord wants us to become saints; that is, we must cheerfully accept all the demands of our state of life, without wanting to escape from the path the Lord has planned for us." (O XII, 214)

Francis proposed that all Christians walk a common road; his ideal of sanctity combined the simplicity of a heart which fears and honors God with an attitude of gentleness toward one's neighbor. This should not be considered a privileged model of sanctity. In his own life, Francis de Sales was the first to carry out the program in detail. Mother Chantal testified that he was constantly abounding in a great interior gentleness which was reflected in his face, and that even when he was alone he was habitually recollected.

If for Francis de Sales sanctity was a divine call valid for everyone, for Don Bosco it was especially so for children and young people. In this perspective, he could simply be described as an educator of youthful sanctity, an incomparable master of this art. Consequently, in his oratory and under his supervision there was a real flowering of young saints, such as Dominic Savio, Francis Besucco and Michael Magone. They incarnated a simple and exemplary holiness—a sanctity wisely modeled on the holy educator—always bearing in mind God's plan and the persons themselves. Each in his own way was a genuine example of holiness, either in the carrying out of resolutions (Savio), or in candor and openness of soul (Besucco), or in the ardor of union with God (Magone). Their sanctity consisted in a joyful spirit and was the fruit of the grace of God. They were different in their personalities, but all alike were joyful in spirit. (See Cornell, W.L., SDB. *Don Bosco: Spiritual Director of Young People.*)

"Rejoice in the Lord always!" (Phil 4:4) was a refrain constantly repeated by all who lived at Don Bosco's side. One of them has rightfully interpreted—as it were, officially—Don Bosco's rule of sanctity: "Here at the oratory we make holiness consist in being very cheerful." (BM V, 228) Grace and serenity must always accompany the carrying out of one's duty, without deviation from the common path. To holy aspirations and good intentions were joined good works and concrete acts.

Ecstasy of Life—Union with God

To tread the path securely and to reach the goal successfully it is indispensible, according to Francis de Sales, to sacrifice one's will and to know how to persevere at carrying out the will of God. God must not be pressured, nor must one try to evade doing what He has in mind.

This type of sanctity is not the fruit of fantasy or of a simple tendency which is too human or unstable. It is sanctity lived out with humility in the routine of daily life, and still more the offering of oneself as ". . . a gift of pleasing fragrance." (Eph 5:2)

With a similar understanding of the Christian and ascetical life, Saint Francis de Sales proposes a short but interesting scenario and points to three of the sacred ecstasies which may take place in human life:

1. The ecstasy of the intellect—visions, raptures and the like which we associate with the lives of the saints.

2. The ecstasy of the will—forms of penance and austere practices associated with those well advanced in perfection.

3. The ecstasy of life or action—works of one's state of life performed out of love; i.e., duty lovingly accomplished in humble, day-to-day living. This applies to most people and is possible for all.

In enumerating these three forms of ecstasy, Saint Francis de Sales clearly prefers the last. The straightforward conclusion is that holiness consists in changing every action into an act of the love of God. This can be done in regard to the most humble of activities. The most modest actions, seemingly of little account and insignificant, if performed out of love, are prized by God. De Sales described this manner of acting in terms all his own—ecstasy of action, or vital prayer:

> The ecstasy totally holy and totally lovable is this one, which crowns the other two. All the actions of those who live in the holy fear of God are continuous prayers. This is called vital prayer. There are many saints in heaven who were never subject to ecstasies of the intellect or the will or to raptures of

contemplation; but we can say with certainty that there are none who had not experience of the ecstasy of life or of action, in the control of self or of their natural inclinations . . . through the practice of an interior gentleness, simplicity and humility, and especially through the practice of charity . . . Then, and only then, do we find the holy ecstasy of divine love, when we live, not according to reason or human inclinations, but beyond them, according to the inspirations and instincts of the divine Savior of our souls. (O IX, 61)

Don Bosco trod the same path; he was an example of ecstasy in action. He may not have used the terminology, but essentially this is what he taught, and he fashioned saints in the process. His life was a prayer, a continual union with God through the exercise of acts performed out of love. Cardinal Alimonda said of him: "Don Bosco was always united with God." He was a man always and fully immersed in a thousand-and-one activities, preoccupied by all sorts of projects, yet continually absorbed in God. His feet were on the ground and his hands on his work, but his heart was fixed on heaven. This was his own way of acting, and this is what he asked of his followers. With a surprising adherence to the circumstances of real life, he left a program of work and temperance. (See pages 72-76.) He believed that work could and should become prayer. Pope Pius XI granted "the indulgence of sanctified work" to the followers of Don Bosco. Don Philip Rinaldi saw in this gesture a confirmation of vital prayer as proposed by Saint Francis de Sales, "the patron of the sanctification of the present moment."[11]

Always in reference to this concept, which is typically Salesian, one can affirm in all truth that apostolic work is the Salesian form of mysticism, because it recognizes its divine and urgent grandeur. One has to be ready for anything if it is a matter of God's glory and the salvation of souls. (P 135) One does not engage in long contemplation but makes up for it by work animated by prayerfulness. The Salesian is asked to perform few practices of piety, but his prayer must be continuous, as the *Salesian Constitutions* state: "Immersed in the world and in the cares of pastoral life, the Salesian learns to meet God through those to whom he is sent." (Art. 95)

Convergence in Practice

Don Bosco's spontaneous gestures reveal his true self more precisely than others' opinions of him or his actions on special occasions. He was firmly convinced that he must faithfully and perseveringly copy his model in everything. This is shown by a simple example, an episode which took place at Borgo San Martino in an institute of the Daughters of Mary Help of Christians.

> [Don Bosco] . . . was offered a cup of coffee with a whipped egg yolk. He accepted it and began putting sugar into it. "Father," the sister simply remarked, "I already put sugar in it!" "Don't you know that Don Bosco must copy the sweetness of Saint Francis de Sales?" he smilingly replied. (BM X, 295)

In speaking about the similarities between Don Bosco and Francis de Sales, we have noted the identity of their asceticism and doctrine. They were also very much alike in the exercise of several virtues. Don Bosco's gentleness and charity made him a living image of the gentle bishop of Geneva. This was the ideal which he first set for himself and then proposed to his followers. He wanted all to be "under the special protection of a saint who had been a perfect model" in this regard. (BM II, 197)

Gentleness and charity: such an ideal of life and of earnest imitation was understood and stressed in one of Don Bosco's dreams. Dew falling from heaven was the symbol of the gentleness of the saint who was his model. As it is related in the dream: "[The dew] . . . signifies the sweetness of the saint whom you have taken as your model. The resemblance to dew means that much effort and sacrifice are needed to maintain such gentleness and that sometimes it can be preserved only by the shedding of one's blood." (BM XIII, 226)

As far as charity is concerned, a good example from among many in Don Bosco's life is at the time of the persecution and expulsion of religious from France. Don Bosco opened the doors of his houses to the Jesuits, who were looking for shelter and moral support in that period of turmoil. Deeply moved, the Jesuit general, Father Beckx, expressed his thanks for the "generous, spontaneous and unconditional offer" in a letter to Don Bosco.

How gracious is our Lord's love! How well was our beloved Saint Francis de Sales imbued by it. How worthily do they bear his name who have so thoroughly inherited his spirit of charity! This is the one of the most consoling benefits which God, in His infinite wisdom, draws from the bitter persecutions which He permits His servants to endure. He inspires good-hearted people to share the sorrows of others and help them at the price of any sacrifice. I do not know if we shall have occasion to accept your generous offer, but I assure you that we shall never forget your generosity, and we shall heartily pray that God will begin to reward you even in this life by blessing, expanding and prospering the zealous works which you and your holy congregation have undertaken for God's greater glory. (BM XIV, 476)

Don Bosco gave us many outstanding examples of how to live the spirit of Saint Francis de Sales. He imitated his model, not only in the way he loved God but also in his love for his neighbor, especially the poor and those most in need—he included young people in this latter category. To these went all his attention and care, particularly in respect to their moral education. Don Ricaldone comments in his *Don Bosco Educator* that the principles of Saint Francis de Sales prompted Don Bosco to lead the young to God by the way of love, and this is the essence of the Salesian spirit.

Don Bosco was so keen to do good that in his meetings with Cooperators he generally chose, as a reading, those passages from the life of Saint Francis de Sales which illustrated his generosity or gave some practical example of his love for the poor and the needy. The ideals of these two great saints seemed to be identical, as brought out by Bishop Mermillot, bishop of Annecy, who addressed a gathering in Turin during a brief stopover between a change of trains on the afternoon of February 23, 1876. As head of the diocese where Francis de Sales had lived, he praised his saintly predecessor while commending Don Bosco, his successor in good works. (cf. BM XII, 90-91)

On this as on other occasions, praise did not affect Don Bosco, who also imitated Saint Francis de Sales in sentiments of humility. The bishop of Geneva, preferring to remain in his small diocese of Annecy, renounced the offer of the Sees of both Paris and Turin and turned down the honor and dignity of the cardinal's hat. Don Bosco likewise had a very humble opinion of himself; he sought neither honors nor office, so that he could remain a humble priest working with his boys.

Don Bosco did not want to be a cardinal or a bishop. Professor John Lorini, at a meeting at Tortona on April 27, 1874, told him of the "great desire in Rome to have him as a cardinal." "Dear professor," Don Bosco replied in his pleasant, half-serious, half-teasing way, "what would I amount to as a cardinal? Nothing at all! Now, at least, as a simple priest I can still do some good." Professor Lorini afterwards wrote that Don Bosco ". . . pressed my hand affectionately, thanking me for my interest in him. Shortly afterward he got into his train and vanished in a cloud of dust and smoke, leaving me his blessing. I can never forget that moment, his words, and that last smile of his." (BM X, 243-244)

The characteristics of the two saints are clearly evident: a humble opinion of oneself, a simple and modest way of acting, and being always available to any reasonable request. Here is another example, small but meaningful: Francis de Sales, on being pressed to have his portrait painted, graciously accepted, almost as if he did not mind how much time he would waste in these endless and tiresome sittings. Referring to this incident, the *Biographical Memoirs* notes Don Bosco's patience in similar circumstances: "When his sons and his friends requested him to let them paint his portrait, imitating even in this the incomparable condescension of de Sales, he did not refuse." (MB XVII, 492)

The imitation of the holy patron resulted from Don Bosco's most ardent desire to acquire a variety of virtues. In this he combined simplicity and straightforwardness, circumspection and foresight. This is shown in a passage from the *Biographical Memoirs* where he is pictured as mindful of the practice of Saint Francis de Sales: "Follow in the footsteps of divine providence; do not lead"—although he sometimes seemed impatient as he waited for the appropriate time. (cf. BM II, 47)

We have chosen only a few examples in the life of Don Bosco. We could continue to list the virtues he shared with his patron, but we recognize, as did so many of his contemporaries, that much of the ascetical or mystical aspects of Don Bosco's life went unnoticed or were taken for granted.

His life was such a wonderful texture of good works, such a shining display of virtues, that it is easy to see in him the figure of Francis de Sales, whose efficacious protection he cherished.

We find an urgent and dramatic appeal in one of the pages of the *Biographical Memoirs*—almost in the form of a last will and testament:

> If the Salesians were really to live their faith as Saint Francis de Sales understood it in his zeal, charity and meekness, I could truly be proud, and there would be reason to hope for a vast amount of good to be done! In fact I might say that the world would come after us, and we would master it. (BM XII, 463)

Similarities in Their Pastoral-Educative Approaches

We also find in the two saints another characteristic and singular affinity; namely, the zeal with which they carried out their apostolate as pastors and educators.

Francis de Sales is commonly called the apostle of the Chablais. The fact that he converted the whole region in a few years was enough to make famous the name of that son of Savoy. Just consider that he was only twenty-seven when he went there in September 1594 and in four years brought back to the Church almost the entire population in a locality so close to Geneva, the bastion of Calvinism. Throughout those four years, despite innumerable difficulties, he was consumed by zeal for the house of the Lord. (cf. Ps 69:10) If his strength was in his faith, his victory was due to his gentle kindness, and the driving force of it all was his apostolic zeal.

That "all things to all men" of the apostle Paul was decisively translated and transformed in the motto of this pastor and bishop, "Taken by God and given to His people," understood as a program for God's honor and the defense of truth. Such an apostolic thrust is seen, above all, in his courage and burning zeal.

If this were the only characteristic which Francis de Sales and Don Bosco shared, that would be enough to show that they were similar souls. Some authors have used it as the basis for an almost exhaustive comparison between the two saints. There is another common ground, however: loyalty to the pope. On this point, Don Bosco has written:

It is my express wish that the members of the humble Congregation of Saint Francis de Sales never depart from the loyalty which this great saint, our patron, had toward the Holy See. They should accept promptly, respectfully and with simplicity of mind and heart not only the decisions of the pope which regard matters of doctrine or discipline, but even in matters which are open to discussion they should always accept his opinion even as a private teacher rather than accept the opinion of some theologian or teacher of the world. (MB XVIII, 277)

Loyalty to the pope was linked with love for the Church; Don Bosco had an ecclesial sense. This was the motivation which prompted the establishment of the Salesian Cooperators, who—according to the program and aim of the founder—would be a prodigious force within the Church. Under the auspices of Saint Francis de Sales, they were to come to the aid of the Church in its most pressing needs. Don Bosco stressed this in speaking to the conference of Cooperators in Turin in June 1885.

The Cooperators engaged in activities and performed good works, always guided by the teachings and directives of the apostle of the Chablais. (These concepts were restated as a rule of action in the presentation of the diploma of Decurion of Cooperators.) Dedicated to the defense of Catholic truth and animated with the Salesian spirit, they were in perfect accord with the various associations which were set up at that time; for example, the catechism of the Catholic Association of Saint Francis de Sales for the Defense and Preservation of the Faith.

8

The Salesian Spirit

Don Bosco kept the distinction between the Salesians, the Daughters of Mary Help of Christians and the Cooperators, but he did not fail to address himself, in a more general fashion, to all of them together. To these, as well as to the youth entrusted to their care, he wanted to hand on that spirit which animated his own way of thinking and acting.

When he used the word Salesian, he meant all who came into contact with his ministry. This included those who had been educated "according to the teaching of Saint Francis de Sales." Referring to priests who were Salesian alumni, he recognized that they were all involved in their own specific mission. Yet in speaking to them on one occasion, he said in a fatherly tone: "My dearly beloved, you received your early education in this very house. You are imbued with the spirit of Saint Francis de Sales and have learned how to help youngsters improve themselves. Fill in for us according to your ability. Come to Don Bosco's aid to attain all the more readily and on a larger scale our noble goals— the welfare of the Church and of civil society—by caring for destitute youngsters." (BM XIV, 402)

We must bear in mind—as Don Ceria points out very well—that in effect:

> More than a doctrine, Don Bosco left behind him a spirit which he inspired among his boys and made of it a living force . . . Only through this personal and persistent work was he able to mold in his own image men who, after his death, held posts of responsibility and planted everywhere the genuine family spirit which they had imbibed at the source . . . Don Bosco, by calling his disciples to his school as helpers who shared with him his fatigues, while he educated them in the principles of religious life, imbued them with a particular spirit which we know as the Salesian spirit. (Annali I, 637, 721)

We note this in passing, but we believe it is important: At a certain point in the history and tradition of the congregation, the spirit of Don Bosco became identified with the Salesian spirit. It is a *constitutive element* of the family created by Don Bosco, which he patiently instilled into the hearts of his first followers and which was finely filtered by a specific way of life and ministry. This spirit was proper to Don Bosco; however, we must not forget that it came to us by way of his holy patron and is very much in line with the practice of the Preventive System, which is totally based on gentle kindness and understanding. Father Auffray has written:

> In giving to his sons the name of the bishop of Geneva, the most gentle person of his century, Don Bosco wished that his spirit of

gentleness, of patience and trusting charity should inspire his works and his methods. He attracted souls to his person by goodness, sacrifice, the understanding of hearts and by the spread of Christian joy. With the maximum of naturalness, he brought souls back to God; such was the method of conversion which the apostle of the Chablais had employed. Saint John Bosco had learned this secret by reading his works and his life. Desirous that his sons should succeed in their work as educators by an all-conquering love, he felt that he could do no better than to put before them, as patron, guide and model, the saint whose name they should bear in the future. (P 77-78)

The title Salesian, whether it refers to an individual who bears this name or to the activities in which he or she is involved, must be carefully preserved and understood. For it relates to the very spirit of Don Bosco and his educational method. This is essentially the message contained in his treatise on *The Preventive System* (1877), based on the practice of gentleness and kindliness. Ultimately it is modeled on the words of Saint Paul: "Love is patient; love is kind . . . There is no limit to love's forbearance, to its trust, its hope, its power to endure." (1 Cor 13:4-7)

Don Bosco was worried that, with the passing of time, the zeal and enthusiasm of his Salesians might lessen. This was the concern that prompted his well-known letter from Rome in 1884. He expressed the same misgivings through a letter written the following year by Father Lazzero, a member of the General Council of the Salesian Congregation. Among other things, fearing that false interpretations could lead to easy compromises or undesirable relaxations with regard to the Preventive System in the Salesian houses of South America, recently opened, he had this to say: ". . . Don Bosco bewails the fact that the spirit of Saint Francis de Sales, which is his spirit, seems to be undergoing a change and insists that this must be the spirit of the congregation in America as elsewhere . . ." (P 79)

Certainly this authoritative statement, preserved in an unedited edition in the Salesian archives, is of the utmost importance. It confirms the significant claim of Father Caviglia who, in comparing the Salesian founder and his patron, asserts that Don Bosco's spirit is the same as that of Saint Francis de Sales. (cf. C IV, 98, 183, 296)

That this is a correct interpretation of the mind of Don Bosco is established by another letter which he wrote to Father Costamagna and the confreres in South America. He appealed to them, with tears, to shy away from all possible deviations in the practice of the Salesian spirit and its traditions. In particular, he emphasized patience as the virtue necessary for all those who work with and for young people. In part, here is what he wrote:

> . . . I would like to give a sermon to all of you or better a conference on the Salesian spirit which must animate and direct all our activities and the accomplishment of our duties. The Preventive System is something which is our very own . . . Every Salesian should be a friend to all; he must never seek revenge; he should be quick to pardon and should not drag up things that have already been pardoned . . . Gentle kindness in speaking and in helping others wins over all hearts. (E IV, 332-333)

This letter had a dramatic effect, an immediate and beneficial reaction, as described in the *Biographical Memoirs*:

> Father Vespignani says that the letter was copied out by many of the confreres; that many felt obliged to thank Don Bosco personally for such a salutary admonition, promising him a scrupulous observance of the Preventive System in the future; that some of them, feeling that they were guilty of a lack of observance or who found it very hard to be charitable and patient, obliged themselves by vow, considered by them as a fourth Salesian vow [a vow of patience], which they renewed every month on the occasion of the Exercise for a Happy Death. (MB XVII, 629)

As can easily be seen, we are in possession of a document of the utmost importance. Nevertheless, to be better informed of the ongoing concern about the Salesian spirit, we should retrace our steps and look at a previous letter dated January 29, 1883. Don Bosco's biographer, Father Ceria, comments that the saint purposely wrote this letter on the feast of Saint Francis de Sales because its theme was the spirit of Francis as an important feature of his own method of education. (cf. E IV, 201)

Developing specific points on the practice of the Preventive System, the letter stressed the need for kindness and gentleness in dealing with the young. The good father cited an example from the life of his patron, recalling how the saint was a model of compassion in dealing with a lad who was rather rebellious and disrespectful. Don Bosco wrote:

> Our dear and kind Saint Francis de Sales, as you know, made a very strict pact with himself not to speak when he was upset. He used to say that he did not want to lose in half an hour that little bit of gentle kindness which had taken him over twenty years to gather up, drop by drop, just as one gathers dew in a jar; a bee takes several months to make a bit of honey which we consume in one mouthful. One day, having been criticized for being too lenient with a young man who had treated his mother in a very nasty way, he said: "This young man was not able to profit from my warnings, because his frame of mind had robbed him of reason and good sense. A harsh correction would have served no purpose whatsoever and would even have been harmful . . ." I bring to your attention these words of our admirable and wise educator of hearts so that you may store them in memory. (E IV, 205-206)

Don Bosco's use of this example from the life of Saint Francis is another confirmation of how he identified his own spirit with that of de Sales. It also shows his familiarity with the saint's life, leading to his choice of him as patron and guide of his apostolic work for youth.

Walking in the Same Spirit

Don Bosco frequently exhorted his followers to the practice of virtue. He made ample use of the shining example of his patron, revealing his own devoted attention to his model. He often focused on the theme of gentle kindness, which was his constant ideal, even from his seminary days. Here are some examples of this recurring theme:

The motto he chose for the year 1880 was "the kindness of Saint Francis de Sales with others." It was directed not only to superiors but to everyone. He himself had always given an example of this in the way he exercised his authority as rector major, making it clear that he understood authority to mean putting oneself at the service of others. This was shown by his effort to understand totally disparate characters, his pardoning mistakes and rude manners, his passing over contradictions and outright refusal to cooperate. In *Alle fonti della vita salesiana*, Don Favini notes: "Don

Bosco, like Saint Francis de Sales, gave a wonderful example of loving kindness . . . Not that everybody corresponded with it! Far from it! He experienced hostility, ingratitude, misunderstandings, hypocrisies, surprises and defections." (P 121)

It was only natural that the superiors, having before them this shining example, tried to copy it. Let us recall what had been suggested to Don Bosco in the dream previously mentioned, where the mysterious guide told him that dew is the symbol of the gentleness of the saint who was his model.

At the end of the narrative of a dream which Don Bosco had at San Benigno on August 30, 1883, we find this thought: "With the gentle kindness of Saint Francis de Sales, the Salesians will bring all the peoples of America to Christ." (MB XVI, 394; cf. also words of Don Rinaldi in ASC 1924, 370.)

As was true for Francis de Sales in the Chablais in the midst of heretics, the efficacy of the missionary apostolate would depend upon this spiritual attitude, especially among people who were ignorant of the Gospel. These apostles would have to make themselves small and humble, giving preferential treatment to the sick, the aged and the young. Bishop Cagliero affirmed that evangelical penetration into the distant lands of Patagonia began with the little ones, the children of the native population, by means of a gentle approach, an openness of heart, a cheerful smile. Don Bosco himself had written: "Insist on the charity and gentle kindness of Saint Francis de Sales, whom we must imitate." (E IV, 340; a letter dated September 30, 1885, to Don Lasagna, who was provincial at the time.)

To gentle kindness must be added, apart from the human requisites, other virtues, especially charity; both are indispensible for the practice of the Preventive System. Don Bosco strongly asserted this in his instructions and meditations during retreats. The tone he employed had more the force of a command than a mere exhortation. ". . . We *must* imitate." It is a pressing invitation addressed to the whole community, all the more timely since it was given during a period of reflection and recollection. However, when Don Bosco spoke to individuals, his tone was that of captivating persuasion. He no longer commanded but quietly offered an urgent but paternal invitation: "Try to exercise the virtues of charity, patience, and the gentle kindness of Saint Francis de Sales." (E IV, 152-153; a letter to Brother Nicholas Fenoglio on July 13, 1882.)

In a style full of foresight and kindly concern, Don Bosco wanted to support the young cleric so as to introduce him to the practice of the Salesian way of life—a wise and helpful initiation.

Besides charity and kindness, anyone working with the young also needs a fair share of patience; this is especially important for a beginner in the field of education. Note that it must be a conscious patience, characterized by full control of oneself, without letup, without surrender. Here we should look at another favorite expression of Don Bosco: "Work but always with the gentleness of Saint Francis de Sales and the patience of Job." (E IV, 196; a letter to Don Dalmazzo, November 26, 1882.)

Every good Salesian must practice this virtue in its typical and proverbial exemplification of the biblical Job, the incarnation of patience. The apostle in the midst of the young needs well-proven energies, especially those of a spiritual nature. Patience must be combined with courage. Don Bosco gave an example of this when he used to say: "If one is to do good, he must have a little courage, be ready for sacrifice, deal affably with all and never slight anybody. By following this method I have always had significant success, in fact, marvelous success." (BM III, 39)

Don Bosco's reminders about the gentleness and kindness of the saint came easily to him: "I know that they will a thousand times be tempted to cut a person down or tell him to get lost or whatever. But this is just the time that he needs vast resources of patience or, better, boundless charity seasoned with Saint Francis de Sales's recipe: kindness and meekness." (BM XII, 329)

This was in a talk he gave to the retreatants at Lanzo in 1876. He also said: "I know how much it costs . . . Believe me, sometimes my blood boils and I am about to burst." His biographer adds this note: "This confession, which reminds us of what Saint Francis de Sales said of his own fiery temperament and his twenty years of effort to control it, is of great value in evaluating Don Bosco's habitual calm even during moments and occasions when such calm appeared impossible to preserve." (ibid., 330)

Following Saint Francis, Don Bosco kept insisting that, as spices are necessary to give taste to food, charity must be seasoned by the practice of patience. This will ensure the successful outcome of every enterprise, especially in the work of the education of the young. With characteristic humility, Don Bosco gives his holy patron credit for his own accomplishments: "Anybody else, even today, could achieve as much [as I have] by emulating the simplicity and gentleness of Saint Francis de Sales." (BM III, 39)

The success of any pastoral activity with boys depends, certainly, on many factors, not the least of which is having faith in one's capabilities. To do good one must be prepared to take risks; there is need of a bit of courageous initiative. Don Bosco had learned this from his mentor. So the sons of Saint Francis de Sales must be open, sincere and simple (in the good sense of the word). Such an attitude will gain the good will of strangers and even of one's very enemies: "If we work with the spirit and zeal of Saint Francis de Sales, the evil forces of the world will have to yield and give way to God's glory and the good of our society." (BM XII, 64)

Tireless Work in the Service of the Church and the Pope

Work and temperance, a motto of Don Bosco's congregation, distinguish the untiring activity of every Salesian who imitates the founder and follows in the footsteps of his patron and protector. Especially in working for the good of the Church, for the triumph of the kingdom of God in the world, Don Bosco took his cue from his patron in unlimited dedication to the cause of the Gospel: "I make my own, from the bottom of my heart, the feelings of faith, esteem, respect, veneration and steadfast love towards the supreme pontiff that characterized Saint Francis de Sales." (MB XVIII, 277)

History and Salesian tradition portray Don Bosco as highly devoted to the pope; "attached to the pope as a limpet to a rock" was his own strong affirmation. We recall his expression of unrelenting faith and devotion, uttered decisively in a moment of trial, even of lamentable opposition:

"I have always remained bound to the Church, and I have never departed from that principle." (P 125)

Don Bosco found in Francis de Sales a marvelous model of fidelity to the Church and to the pontiff.

Renewal in the Salesian Spirit

In concluding this chapter on the Salesian spirit, we can do no better than recall the founder's express intentions. At the beginning of the first general chapter of the Salesian Society in September 1877, after the public and solemn invocation of the Sacred Heart, of Mary most holy and of Saint Francis de Sales, Don Bosco declared: "Saint Francis of Sales, our patron, will also preside over our meetings and will hopefully obtain the help we need from God to make our deliberations in keeping with his spirit." (BM XIII, 183)

Almost one hundred years later, the Salesians of Don Bosco met in a special general chapter (the twentieth),[12] convened for renewal in the light of the Second Vatican Council. They recalled that the bishop of Geneva was Don Bosco's model of zeal for souls, of the defense of truth, of fidelity to the Catholic Church, and above all else of a completely evangelical method of exercising this zeal: "charity, sweetness, courtesy, great calm, extraordinary gentleness," as Don Bosco himself expressed it. (cf. MO 141; *Regulation for the Oratory*, 1877, 4)

They then declared their allegiance to the pastoral method of Saint Francis de Sales and his spirit of optimism and joy. In the acts of the chapter, the Salesian spirit and method are set forth as follows:

Method of the Good Shepherd

Inspired by the Spirit who wants to conform him to Christ—meek and humble of heart—the Salesian chooses love as the means and fundamental method of his apostolate, conscious of its demands of friendly contacts, patience, and death to oneself, but also of the victorious strength of the Risen One.

In this light he perceives more clearly the pastoral method of Saint Francis de Sales by which Don Bosco was inspired, the promoter of untiring affection and of familiarity—Salesian names for love applied to young people. It becomes clear how much the method of the two saints was directly inspired by the Christ of the Gospels who appeared among us as "the kindness and love of God . . ." (Ti 3:4) It is the image of Christ the Good Shepherd (cf. Jn 10:14-15) that today's Salesian is particularly aware of.

The movement towards friendly dialogue with all men, brought about by the Church of today, drives the Salesian to a stronger commitment to his own characteristic method. It is in this ecclesial and Salesian context that we find our fidelity to an educative style which Don Bosco himself called the Preventive System.

Optimism and Joy

"Let nothing upset you! Be cheerful!" said Don Bosco on many occasions. The true Salesian never lets himself be discouraged by the difficulties he encounters: Believe all things, hope all things, endure all things. (cf. 1 Cor 13:7) His optimistic humanism, inspired by Saint Francis de Sales, enables him to appreciate all that is human and to have confidence in the natural and supernatural resources of man, while not being blind to human weakness, especially where youth is concerned. He knows how to gather and to appreciate the values present in the world and in history. He refuses to grumble about his own times. He holds on to all that is good (cf. 1 Thes 5:21), especially if it is liked by young people.

In a lifestyle that is single in its outlook and its contacts, he nurtures a permanent sense of joy—a necessary gift for the educator of the young—and expresses, within the limits of possibility, a happy disposition; but more than that, he expresses a radiant faith: ". . . the fruit of the spirit is love, joy, peace . . ." (Gal 5:22) In today's world in which young people often become skeptical, sad and sometimes despairing, or even naively optimistic about their future, the joy of a Salesian, with all its realism, seems to give encouragement to the first group and to lead the second group to a realistic awareness of things.

9

The Salesianity of Don Bosco

Father Eugene Valentini, SDB, has spoken and written extensively on the Salesian spirit and on Don Bosco's spirituality.[13] In this chapter we will summarize his thoughts on the subject.

A clarification is necessary. By spirituality we mean neither spiritual theology nor spiritual doctrine, but a style or way of the spiritual life lived to an eminent degree and proper to an institution or an individual. Every saint has a spirituality indicative of his or her way of thinking, speaking or acting. Similarly, every congregation or religious order has its own spiritual life or spirituality.

Francis de Sales, as a saint, founder and writer, was the author of a new spirituality—Salesian—which influenced many people and so became a school of spirituality. The same can be said of Don Bosco; while following in the footsteps of the great bishop of Geneva, he had his own distinct personality. Likewise, the congregation he founded had such originality and fecundity as to have a following in its own right.

If it is true that a founder creates a new form of the spiritual life, so vibrant that it spreads a new lifestyle of holiness, then we must attribute to that life and vitality the glorious title of a school of spirituality. As the Second Vatican Council teaches, a school of holiness flourishes anew within the Church when a new religious congregation emerges under the inspiration of the Holy Spirit. The Spirit breathes wherever and however He wills, enriching the mantle of His spouse with ever-new flowers of virtue, from the most hidden and humble to the most resplendent and widespread.

God creates neither saints nor institutions according to one set pattern; each has a mission and a particular makeup. Children resemble their parents, but they are not an exact replica of them. So Don Bosco, while sharing to a large extent the features of Saint Francis de Sales (since he was inspired by him and sought to transplant his spirit into the institution he was founding), is not a photographic image of him. Differences of time, education, mission and talents led to the development of a new type of holiness.

What are the characteristics of the spirituality of Saint Francis de Sales? Which of these have been incorporated into the spirituality of Don Bosco?

These are questions to which there is no easy answer. A fundamental reason for this difficulty is that life can never be completely reduced to a series of formulae. Another lies in the richness and complexity of Salesian spirituality, which, because of its many facets, cannot be taken in at a single glance. Therefore we must limit ourselves to a consideration of some of the more salient features of the spirituality of Saint Francis de Sales and see how these are reproduced, or perhaps modified, in the spirituality of Don Bosco.

Flexibility

Salesian spirituality is human, vital and concrete, not that of a functionary but of a man or woman of action. This is typical of modern spirituality, which is attracted more to reality than to theory, abstract methods or the experiences of the past. People today want an active and dynamic apostolate unrestricted by complex rules. No one wants a spirituality that is too rigid or exacting.

Saint Francis de Sales had already thrown open doors and windows, letting in the fresh air of liberty that was practically unknown at his time. This free spirit was particularly noticeable in his concept of obedience and in his method of prayer. On obedience he wrote:

> Here is the general rule of our obedience written in capital letters: LOVE AND NOT FORCE SHOULD INSPIRE ALL THAT YOU DO; LOVE OBEDIENCE MORE THAN FEAR DISOBEDIENCE. I want you to have a spirit of liberty, not the kind that excludes obedience, for that is the liberty of the flesh, but the kind that excludes constraint and scruples or overeagerness . . . We must act on the minds of others as the angels do, graciously and without coercion . . . My ideas are summed up in the words "gentle encouragement." (O XII, 359; letter 234)

On prayer, he wrote that many make the mistake of believing that a detailed method is required to pray well, and they hunt high and low to find a certain art for praying in the best possible way, analyzing many systems that are proposed. "I do not say that these methods have no value, but I do say that a person ought not to get too attached to them." (O VI, 347)

On a number of occasions the saint expressed pity for those poor people who torture themselves seeking the art of loving God, not realizing that there is no art besides that of loving Him. They try to discover the secret of perfection and then hope that it will come automatically. They are only fooling themselves. Perfection consists in the union of our soul with the divine goodness; it suffices to know little and to do much.

Jean Pierre Camus, the saint's faithful interpreter, puts it this way: "If a person is invited to a lavish banquet and wants to taste something from every dish, he ends up with a bloated stomach and a horrible attack of indigestion. The same thing happens to those people who want to test every means and every method that could possibly lead them to perfection." (Camus, Jean Pierre. *The Spirit of Saint Francis de Sales*, 38)

Paraphrasing the saint's thought, Camus places these words on his lips: "Many ask me for methods, means and secrets of perfection, and I reply that I know of no other perfection except that of loving God with all one's heart and our neighbor as ourselves. The whole secret of acquiring this love lies in loving; as one, by studying, learns to study, by speaking learns to speak, by running learns to run, and by working learns to work, so one learns to love by loving. If anyone tries to follow any other method, he makes an utter fool of himself." (ibid., 1)

This is truly a Salesian principle, a principle followed by Don Bosco throughout his life. He trained his followers to become educators by plunging them into the work and supporting them by advice and correction. He used to say that by throwing them into the water they learned to swim. He himself had absorbed this lesson in his first dream when the august personage told him: "So begin right now to show them that sin is ugly and virtue beautiful." His spiritual life was lived first of all and then taught to his Salesians, staying clear at all times from any predetermined method.

Don Philip Rinaldi, in his *strenna* for 1930, made the following comment to the Salesian Sisters:

Not obstructive methods or cumbersome formulae but an evangelical simplicity: clear the path of so many obstacles that prevent unity, the obstacles of sin and bad habits, abruptly and decisively, without getting all worked up about them; and then straightaway begin to walk along the track so cleared, performing acts of love, accepting sacrifices that we may meet in the carrying out of our mission. Copying Don Bosco, we must be united with God by the shortest and least time-consuming method, by consecrating to Him all the good we do for others, which is the real proof of our love of God and of our union with Him.

This thought of Father Rinaldi was but an echo of that of Don Paul Albera:

Founders of religious institutions aim, in the first place, at personal sanctification and only then turn to working for others. Therefore, he who wishes to become a member of an institute must, above all, consecrate many years to personal sanctification. Don Bosco, however, with a fine understanding of the spirit of his time, was uneasy with certain nonessential, detailed methods to reach this goal, and he understood that with a little good will one can grow in sanctity side by side with being engaged in the works of the apostolate. (L 365)

Don Bosco had another reason for acting in this way, and that was the environment in which he worked—among the young, who want to be on the move but lack experience and strength to sustain their activity with any degree of constancy. They find it difficult to work if the manner of acting is too detailed or demanding. Childhood and youth are times of development, discovery, creativity, ideals and a variety of experiences, and in this atmosphere only the lively and the flexible have any chance of success.

Spirituality in Action

In the past, people were a little afraid of this term; today, after Vatican II, such diffidence has disappeared or at least is tending to disappear.

In the *Decree on the Apostolate of the Laity*, we find this clear statement:

Family cares should not be foreign to their [lay people's] spirituality, nor any other temporal interest; in the words of the apostle, "Whatever you do, whether in speech or in action, do it in the name of the Lord Jesus. Give thanks to God the Father through him." (Col 3:17)

With these words the council has practically canonized the spiritual doctrine of Saint Francis de Sales. For if spirituality means that life is lived in an eminent manner with a constant striving for perfection, then action, which is proper to this life, cannot be excluded. In a broad sense, action encompasses both thought and speech; however, it is more commonly understood to be the opposite of thinking and speaking. In the strictest sense, by spirituality of action we mean apostolic activity of any kind, whether it be that of priests, religious or lay people.

Apostolic action is properly missionary and embraces all activities and duties of a pastoral or missionary nature. If we want to go even deeper into the question, we must say that such activities and duties must also be considered as a means to perfection, because they are incarnations, as Masure says, of charity toward our neighbor. We come to realize this only when we succeed in seeing God present in all the circumstances of life. Every event and every person is the bearer of a divine message and is at the same time an invitation to complete some mission. To accomplish this mission, in ourselves and in others, we must know how to combine contemplation with action so that we become, like Saint Francis de Sales and Don Bosco, contemplatives in action. These saints, while they worked, continually saw God in people and people in God, and they immolated themselves in exterior and continuous work which was imbued with a supernatural spirit.

Many Christians, fearful of falling into the heresy of action, have failed to understand this reality; yet even in his time Saint Augustine explained that there are many ways of following the injunction of Psalm 146: "Sing with your way of living so that you never remain silent . . . Therefore if you wish to praise God, do not sing only with your tongue but also make use of the psalter of good works as a musical instrument. You must praise God while you go about your business . . . while you rest in bed, while you sleep; and when is it that you cannot praise Him?"

Saint Thomas Aquinas, in his commentary on the Epistle to the Romans (Rom 1:9-10), remarks: "A man prays so long as he tends towards God with his heart, voice and work, and so he who orders all his life towards God prays at all times."

Saint Francis de Sales said that in this life we must nourish a prayer of works and of deeds. He was a man of action who believed that life is worth living. Such a life must be lived, however, with rectitude of intention, because intention is the soul of action. Someone once posed to Francis the question of whether a religious who lived an active life gained more merit than one who followed a contemplative life. He answered that contemplation unites us to God more immediately than action; all the same, in the present and often pressing necessities of this life, action has many advantages over contemplation. In the final analysis, those gain more merit who work or contemplate with the greater degree of love. (Camus, op. cit., 211)

Francis held that there is no need to forego the exercise of prayer unless it is to attend to more important works; then one must make up for that omission with frequent aspirations. While one prays it is essential never to forget to make some good resolution, since this is the fruit of prayer.

It was his conviction that no occupations are distracting except those that separate us from God, and only sin separates us from God; every lawful enterprise is a means to unite us to Him more closely. For Saint Francis de Sales it is a manifest error to think that lawful occupations can drive a wedge between ourselves and God. On the contrary, there is no stronger cement binding us to God than that of doing everything for His greater glory. To turn our back on our duties in order to devote ourselves to God by prayer, solitude, reading, silence, recollection, repose or contemplation would be to abandon God to unite ourselves with ourselves and our self-love.

The carrying out of our duties and work for the salvation of souls are an exercise and a test of our love for God. Don Bosco was thinking along these lines when he made work one of the mainsprings of his spirituality. He often recommended to his boys, not severe penances and discipline, but persevering effort in the accomplishment of duty.

This was a constant refrain of Don Bosco in speaking not only to his boys but to his Salesians. He seemed to recommend work more often than prayer. Father Caviglia notes: "Ninety percent of his discourses to his confreres dealt with work, temperance and poverty. This was a sort of scandal— the scandal of a saint who in this regard might be called

'American'—he advised us to work more often than he advised us to pray!"[14]

Pope Pius XI, who knew and canonized the saint, was not scandalized. He called Don Bosco's devotion to work a "martyrdom" for the Lord. He spoke of this in the discourse delivered in the courtyard of Saint Damascus the day after the beatification of Don Bosco. It was this same pope who, some years before, had granted to the venerable servant of God, Father Rinaldi, the indulgence for sanctified labor when he said that work can truly become prayer, provided that it is properly motivated. (cf. Rinaldi, Peter. *By Love Compelled*, 29)

What kind of work is prayer? It is certainly not work plain and simple without any interior intention. Prayer is the elevation of the mind and heart to God. We can do this by thinking lovingly of Him, for example, in mental prayer. Vocal prayer is also the elevation of the mind and heart to God, but expressed in words.

There is a prayer which we might call *vital prayer*; it is performed by works instead of words. This singular phenomenon occurs when the supernatural intention of the one who works permeates all that he or she does with such purity and to such an extent that it divinizes it. In this case, the intention becomes the very purpose of the work itself. Then the action is no longer sanctified by ejaculations that accompany it; rather, the ejaculations are an effect of sanctified work. The apostle, through his or her work, adores, gives thanks, petitions, offers and makes reparation. Realizing the importance of work, he or she unites to it a prayer to obtain God's intervention, that it may be beneficial for the salvation of souls.

This mystical and supernatural attitude during work is the perfection and culmination of what Saint Francis de Sales wrote about in his *Treatise on the Love of God*. He considered the habit of ejaculatory prayer to be the heart of all devotion. It can make up for one's inability to spend long hours in meditative prayer, but if it is missing, nothing else can make up for it.

This same thought is found in Article 15 of the *Constitutions* written by Don Bosco: "Each one shall, besides his vocal prayers, make no less than half an hour's mental prayer every day, unless prevented from doing so by the calls of his sacred ministry. In that case, he shall make up the deficiency by more frequent ejaculations and by directing to God with greater fervor and devotion those particular labors which are thus hindering him from the ordinary practices of piety."

Francis Hermans, in his *Histoire doctrinale de l'humanisme chrétien*, gives preeminence to Saint Francis de Sales among all the great humanists and the heralds of the mystique of work. Hermans fails to mention Don Bosco. Yet the latter, following Saint Francis de Sales, is perhaps unsurpassed in placing so much importance on the value of work in the formation of a person, a Christian and a saint. He made work one of the characteristic elements of his spirituality, recognizing its function in the perfecting of civilization, underlining its positive and formative role in creating an earthly paradise, and making of it an instrument of penance and of redemption in the temptations and difficulties of life.

Don Philip Rinaldi, interpreting Don Bosco's mind, emphasized the fact that our Savior redeemed us not only by the shedding of his blood but also by his daily work.

Signs of Don Bosco's Spirit

In his annual message of 1915, Don Paul Albera took up the matter of the sacrifice involved in practicing the Salesian spirit. He proposed four resolutions which, if practiced, would be signs of that spirit:

I will keep God ever before me.
Jesus shall be my model.
Mary shall be my aid.
I shall be the victim.

Then he asked a question for each person to answer individually: Would you like to know if you really have the spirit of Don Bosco? Examine yourself carefully on these three points:

1. Am I constantly serene and cheerful?
2. Am I pleasant and patient in my dealings with my neighbor?
3. Do I live as a victim ever ready for sacrifice?

I hope that your conscience allows you to answer yes to each one of these questions.

No single statement or treatise can be the last word on the Salesian spirit of Don Bosco. Referring to the summary of the twentieth general chapter of the Salesians (see pages 67-68), Father Martin McPake has commented that it would be a mistake to think that these pages on the Salesian spirit constitute an exhaustive, definitive statement. (*A Simple Commentary on the Constitutions*, 99) This view is confirmed by the authoritative Father John Futrell, S.J., who says that in dealing with charisms we are not at the level of law or historical fact but at the level of mystery—a gift of the Spirit; our formulations can never be final or binding.

In the words of Father John Ayers, SDB: "Having humbly admitted the ongoing pilgrim-search for our *anima Salesiana*, we are still urgently required to posit some living principle of cohesion to hold the entire Salesian project of Don Bosco together. And there is overwhelming evidence to show that this broad, liberal *anima Salesiana* is Salesianity—the life, spirit and teaching of Francis de Sales as intended and interpreted by Don Bosco."

Such Salesianity is not a barrier separating the present from the past nor the past from the future, nor the Salesians of Don Bosco from the various groups within the Church that have been inspired by Saint Francis de Sales. Salesianity is vast and complex, and its primary source is Sacred Scripture. Francis de Sales is the gentle, scriptural guide expressly chosen by Don Bosco and others to lead us through the relevant love-themes of the Gospel that manifest love or visible goodness. Such was the *bontà* (gentle goodness) spoken of in John Bosco's first dream. In each new age, variations on the theme do not weaken but intensify this Salesianity.

Again Father Ayers writes:

The only infallible index of authentic Christian and religious life, Salesian-wise, still remains that of Francis's *Introduction* and *Treatise*: patient self-sacrifice and charity pleasantly at work. This is the perennial bond with Salesianity. Salesian bonding does not detract one iota from Don Bosco's originality, as Father Ceria has explained. Don Bosco's genius lies in *non nova sed noviter*, a strength in prompt improvisation rather than in scholarly invention. His originality is kept safe and intact at an entirely different level of pastoral practice rather than of ascetical theory.

The very same Salesian bond makes as one Don Bosco's educational method and his spirituality . . . So at the theological level, the interconnecting thread that runs through both educational and religious lifestyle is precisely Salesianity as our bonding spirit of unity, with its climactic ecstasy of action.

Father Egidio Viganò, rector major of the Salesians, has shown the young Cooperators how this Salesian apex is found side by side in Francis's *Treatise* and in Teresa of Avila's *Interior Castle*:

If the heart stays close with the Lord, it should forget itself entirely; so forgetful of self that one's mind is totally taken up with pleasing Him and with discovering new ways to express one's love for Him . . . This spiritual nuptial is constantly giving birth to good works. We pray not to enjoy it, but with the aim of gathering fresh energy to serve the Lord. Martha and Mary must keep in step, for true hospitality must also give the Lord something to eat. For the soul of prayer is charity, always on the lookout for providential opportunities to act or to suffer so that it can please the Lord. (Interior Castle 4, 8)

Teresa's highest or seventh mansion of prayer is identical with Francis's apex of operative charity.

There is no speculative treatise on such Salesianity from the hand of Don Bosco. But there was an oft-traveled path from Turin to Annecy in Don Bosco's constant spiritual pilgrimage to help implement, in practice, his great Salesian dream: a lived and living synthesis of Salesianity.

If one is to do good, he must have a little courage, be ready for sacrifice, deal affably with all and never slight anybody. By following this method I have always had significant success, in fact, marvelous success. Anybody else, even today, could achieve just as much by emulating the simplicity and gentleness of Saint Francis de Sales. (BM III, 39)

Today, as in the past, as a confidence booster we should turn to that great, magnanimous reservoir so consistently tapped and recommended by Don Bosco. The whole Salesian family will benefit in practice from these prophetic waters of Francis de Sales, fed from the living, never-ending fountainhead of Christ's Gospel.

PART III

The Final Years and Aftermath

Patterns Are Integrated

10

Chief Expressions of Don Bosco's Devotion to Saint Francis de Sales

From Imitation to Devotion

Don Bosco not only imitated Saint Francis de Sales and shared his spirit. In very definite ways he sought to live out his devotion and make it manifest to his followers. He had providentially come to know the saint and therefore to love him. This love found expression particularly in the annual celebration of his feast, the timely distribution of his writings and some significant gestures which occurred in determined circumstances in the life of the holy founder. Throughout the period of Don Bosco's maturity—the period of his greatest activity, when his holiness became more apparent—he continued to be guided by his "dear and gentle" saint.

Annual Celebration of the Feast of Saint Francis de Sales

The liturgical celebrations in the Church calendar did not prevent Don Bosco from writing biographies of saintly youths who were his contemporaries, known to him personally for their holiness of life, who had already been called to eternity. These he presented to his boys for their imitation. Nevertheless, his love for his traditional and canonized patrons was not diminished.

From the very beginning of his work, Don Bosco left in the regulations of the oratory a genial prescription which merits attention. These regulations clearly prescribe that the feasts of Saint Francis de Sales and of Saint Aloysius are to be kept with particular pomp and solemnity.

The *Biographical Memoirs* are rich in early references, among which is the following: "Things began to take shape in the new festive oratory . . . The name of Saint Francis de Sales was becoming a household name, and at the very outset Don Bosco determined to have the feast day of this amiable saint celebrated with all solemnity." (BM II, 196)

A pressing invitation was extended to the boarders of the oratory and then to the other houses that there should be "a special devotion to Saint Francis de Sales." From this it appears that it was Don Bosco's intention to present de Sales as a model not only for Salesians and future Salesians but for the boys themselves. Even they should be or learn to become Salesians by striving to be sincerely devoted to the saint and imitate him. Among the recommendations for all the students there was an invitation to read not only the life of Saint Francis de Sales but also, from his written works, his *Letters*, to learn the art of writing well.

In later years, the *Biographical Memoirs* reports the following injunction: "The feast of Saint Francis de Sales should be celebrated in all of our houses as solemnly as possible. At the oratory it should be celebrated on the feast day itself (January 29) and, in the other houses, on the following Sunday." (MB X, 1115; Italian version, omitted in the English edition.)

For the celebration of the year 1876, here are Don Bosco's own words addressed to his boys:

Saint Francis de Sales is our patron saint, the namesake of the oratory. That's why we call it "the Oratory of Saint Francis de Sales." We ought to celebrate this feast with all possible solemnity and devotion. Let each one strive to draw full personal spiritual profit from it. As for all other novenas, I again strongly ask that each one keep his conscience free of sin so as to be able to receive communion daily. However, as regards frequent reception of the Eucharist, each of you should consult his confessor and do as he says. But the thing that you must never forget is to keep your conscience always in such condition that you may receive communion daily. (BM XII, 18)

After some advice for the smooth running of the house, in a very simple style, he went on to particulars:

Now what shall I suggest to honor our patron saint? As you know, Saint Francis de Sales is the saint of meekness and patience. During this novena I would like all of you to strive to imitate these virtues . . . as a nosegay I suggest that during the novena you endure cold, dampness and other discomforts without complaint in honor of Saint Francis [de Sales]. When you have to suffer illness, insults or other hurts just say: "I'll offer it up for the love of God." The Lord will be very pleased and through our patron saint's intercession will bless you. If anyone would like to do something else equally good he may do so, especially if he strives to imitate our saint in observing silence and self-control and in speaking with concern for his companion's feelings . . . Let each one resolve to be more diligent in doing his work. (BM XII, 20-21)

We find similar expressions on a much earlier occasion (January 19, 1865): "The Saint Francis's novena begins tomorrow. I am not going to suggest special acts of devotion, I want you to be more precise exact in keeping the house rules . . . Our holy patron will know how to reward you." (BM VIII, 15)

Some of the practices in vogue to celebrate the feast of the patron saint were ingenious. Don Bosco would get a prominent person to sponsor the event as a patron or prior, taking the occasion for a solemn distribution of prizes to students. At that ceremony those who deserved rewards were singled out, in a totally democratic way because the names of the boys as well as those of the clerics were read. All were considered and treated on an equal basis in the house of Don Bosco.

There was great enthusiasm. One such scene is described by a modern commentator, paraphrasing the *Biographical Memoirs*:

From the time when the first regulations were proclaimed at the festive oratory, Don Bosco gave the reason why Saint Francis de Sales was chosen as patron . . . and from the very first years of the boarding school, as was done at the oratory, the feast of the patron saint was celebrated with great solemnity. For some time there was a procession with a statue of the saint ... For the boarders more still was done. His feast day was set down for the giving of prizes for good conduct for all resident students. And this was conducted in a special way: throughout the preceding week every student wrote down on a piece of paper the name of the companion he considered the best behaved and gave these papers to Don Bosco. Those who received the most nominations were given prizes on the evening of the feast in a solemn ceremony in the presence of the superiors and the students ... Let us consider the educational worth of this prize-giving, seeing the conduct of both boys and clerics in the light of the most gentle patron. The initiatives of Don Bosco! ... The family atmosphere reflected the spirit of Saint Francis de Sales. (Favini, *Alle fonti della vita Salesiana*, 233-235; P 86)

Other external manifestations—on similar occasions— gave a joyous and fraternal tone to the celebration shared by the Salesians, the past pupils and Cooperators. All made use of the festivities—and even used them as a pretext at times—to honor both the founder and the patron. Such was the case, for example, when Bishop Alimonda, bishop of Albenga and a great admirer of Don Bosco, was the preacher for the feast. We find details of his panegyric in the *Biographical Memoirs* reported from the chronicle of the house of Alassio:

... the bishop [Bishop Cajetan Alimonda] had gone to the school to deliver the panegyric of Saint Francis de Sales on February 2. On that occasion he had spoken lovingly of Don Bosco:

What shall I say of you, Don Bosco, my dearest friend, reverend father of our clergy? You first came to know of Saint Francis de Sales when you were a young boy, and you drank in his gentle wisdom, his charming holiness, his full array of kindly, Christlike virtues which you so much honor. From him you drew the concept of the Salesian Congregation and its spirit ... In you Saint Francis de Sales lives on and multiplies himself, as he does throughout the world ... (BM XIV, 34)

The two saints—even in those times—were not only remembered with love but were put in the same category as regards merits and virtue, and as we have already pointed out were almost identical as far as the preciousness of their messages was concerned.

Annual Meeting of Rectors on the Occasion of the Feast

Another event of capital importance occurred on the feast of Saint Francis de Sales. Don Bosco used this feast as a very suitable occasion to bring together all those responsible for his Salesian houses. They were called, as if to a summit meeting, to add to the solemnity. For example, in 1865: "As usual, but more solemnly than before, the prescribed annual conference took place for all the Salesians. Don Bosco presided over the meeting . . . After praising and thanking his co-workers, he briefed them on what had been done at the oratory. He exhorted them to promote the festive oratories, assuring them of the protection of the madonna." (BM VIII, 16)

The most important meeting occurred in March 1869 just after Don Bosco had returned from Rome, having received the decree approving his society and authorizing him to issue the so-called dimissorial letters for its members. The *Biographical Memoirs* highlights the joyous atmosphere of this occasion:

All the windowsills and balconies flickered with lights arranged into artistic patterns and into inscriptions hailing Saint Francis de Sales and Don Bosco. Night prayers were said in the study hall. After the boys had retired, the Salesians and postulants gathered in the dining room to hear Don Bosco . . . He then went on to describe to his eager Salesians what he had done in order to obtain the coveted approval . . . He enumerated the seemingly insurmountable difficulties that stood in his way and described our Lady's interventions to win over to his cause those prelates who felt they could not consent to certain demands of his. He declared that these interventions had been more effective than any argument, and he recalled the fatherly affection with which the pope had received him. He then thanked God for the Church's approval of his society and enumerated the favors and indulgences which had been granted to him. Finally, underscoring the importance of the decree of March 1, he remarked: In approving our congregation, the Holy Father went well beyond my expectations. I received ten times as much as I had anticipated. These are the main results:

1. The Society of Saint Francis de Sales is definitively approved.

2. Boys who enter the oratory or any of the schools prior to their fourteenth year are exempt from episcopal jurisdiction. The superior general therefore may issue dimissorial letters for them, thus dispensing with their bishops' permission for ordination. As for those members of our society who entered houses after their fourteenth year, we shall simply have to send their names to Rome, and the Holy See will issue dimissorials for them . . .

So now you know why I went to Rome and what I did there. We have obtained exemptions and privileges, but we shall always be very obedient to our bishops and pastors and shall not avail ourselves of privileges, except when all other means, even those that may require humility on our part, have failed. As for the rest, let us thank God with all our heart. With His assistance may our society sanctify itself individually and collectively, thus bringing forth worthy fruits for the glory of God and the welfare of souls. In this way we shall make ourselves beloved and perform great deeds in God's name. (BM IX, 261-263)

Annual Conferences of Salesian Cooperators

Don Bosco's attention was restricted neither to the oratory nor to the congregation; his sphere of influence was much wider. He sought to make his work even more effective through his Salesian Cooperators, creating with wise foresight the atmosphere of a large family. He made this project a reality first of all with a group of lay people who initially bore the name of the Association (or Associates) of the Society of Saint Francis de Sales. This was a branch later grafted into the vital trunk of the same family, joined to it by a spiritual link recognized by the Church. To bind it closely to the congregation, conferences or convocations were held.

All who belonged to the association were invited to these conferences, scheduled as a general rule for the feasts of Mary Help of Christians (May 24) and of Saint Francis de Sales (January 29). We know of at least seventy-nine conferences Don Bosco gave to his Cooperators, twenty-eight of which took place in France.[15] The early issues of the *Salesian Bulletin* and the *Biographical Memoirs* transmit the record of some fifty conferences, and they also provide us frequently with the text.

The meeting became commonly known as the annual conference and had as its aim to acquaint people with the most urgent task facing the congregation, i.e., the education of young people. In the mind of Don Bosco, the Cooperators should work in close collaboration with the Salesians and for the same goals, while remaining in the world and living with their families. He counted on them most of all for their support of his educational projects. These meetings were conducted to give his Cooperators guidelines. In addition, beginning in 1876, on the occasion of the feast of Saint Francis de Sales, Don Bosco sent a circular letter to the Cooperators scattered here and there. In this way, if it was impossible for them to attend meetings, they would feel well-informed and morally united, as in a family. (cf. BM XIII, 470)

There also evolved a pattern for proceeding and for conducting devout practices. In one of these programs we find: "The conference shall commence with the usual reading of a chapter of the life of Saint Francis de Sales, followed by the singing of a hymn . . ." (*Salesian Bulletin* 1880). It is also interesting to read a booklet composed by Don Dalmazzo in 1890 entitled: *A Devout Exercise Proposed for Salesian Cooperators for the Feast of Their Glorious Patron, Saint Francis de Sales.* This seemed to be an opportune moment to learn a bit more about their patron and his teachings. Don Bosco himself set the example, quoting extracts or episodes which had as their aim to put before the Cooperators the saint as a model of apostolic zeal.

An incident brings to light the informal way in which these annual meetings were held. At the meeting in 1879, ". . . the procedure was the usual one, except that the reading from the life of Saint Francis de Sales was replaced by a reading from the biography of Saint Jane Frances de Chantal that described her husband's tragic death and her heroic patience as she dedicated the rest of her life entirely to God's service and to works of charity." (BM XIV, 96)

On another occasion, April 21, 1887, the opening of the Cooperators' conference at Genoa, we read: "The ceremony got under way immediately. A student from Sampierdarena read an extract from the life of Saint Francis de Sales." (MB XVIII, 304)

This, then, was the customary format for the opening of the meeting: sometimes extracts from the *Introduction* were read, and sometimes maxims were taken from the many collections then in circulation or from the life of the saint itself. The most popular life at the time was that written by Canon Gallizia (1737) when he was chaplain of the Convent of the Visitation in Turin. Perhaps this was the one best known to Don Bosco.

In certain respects there was nothing out of the ordinary in these practices; they were those generally followed in the various confraternities scattered throughout Italy and especially in Piedmont, as we have already seen. Yet there was something special about them. Don Bosco desired that the utmost fervor be aroused for these occasions, as we read in the *Catholic Readings* of January 1880, which bear this title: "A Devout Homage Proposed to Salesian Cooperators on the Occasion of the Feast of Saint Francis de Sales."

The pious union accepted women as well as men. While initially it was Don Bosco's intention to set up a union-sodality for men only, he humbly changed his views at the specific invitation of Pius IX. (cf. BM XIV, 96) He gave credit for the inclusion of women to the Holy Father, the pope of the Immaculate Conception and an outstanding benefactor, a man and a saint with an extraordinary devotion to Saint Francis de Sales and a lover of his spirituality.

The Salesian Cooperators Today

Over one hundred years have passed since Don Bosco wrote the first *Constitutions of the Salesian Cooperators* (1876). In the revised *Constitutions* published in 1986, the spirit of the original is retained. Chapter four deals with the Salesian spirit. Article twenty-eight emphasizes the central place of apostolic love, implied in the name Salesian and derived from the patron, Saint Francis de Sales, "model of amiability, apostolic zeal and true humanism." Article thirty-five deals with the preferred devotions of the Salesian Cooperator: Mary Help of Christians, Saint Joseph, Saint John Bosco and Saint Francis de Sales, together with the canonized and beatified members of the Salesian family.

Salesian Family Album

*Shown on these pages are selected paintings
and photographs of Saint Francis de Sales and
Don Bosco, of people who worked with them
during their lifetimes, and others who promoted devotion to these two saints or founded religious orders inspired by their spirituality.
While pictures could not be obtained of all of
them, this representative sample gives us some
idea of the influence of the Salesian spirit even
to the present day.*

*The editor is grateful to the Oblates of Saint
Francis de Sales, the Missionaries of Saint
Francis de Sales, the Salesian Communica-
tions Office and the Sisters of the Visitation for
permission to use the pictures presented here.*

The Altar of the Religious Founders in the Basilica of Mary Help of Christians in Turin. Saint John Bosco and Saint Francis de Sales stand in the center. From left to right are Saint Francis of Assisi, Saint Dominic, Saint Benedict, Saint Philip Neri, Saint John Baptist de la Salle and Saint Ignatius Loyola. The inscription below the arch is the Salesian motto: "Give me souls; take away the rest."

Official portrait of Saint Francis de Sales painted in 1618

Actual photograph of Don Bosco taken in 1880

Saint Jane Frances de Chantal, co-foundress with Saint Francis de Sales of the Order of the Visitation

Saint Mary Mazzarello, co-foundress with Don Bosco of the Daughters of Mary Help of Christians

Blessed Michael Rua, first successor of Don Bosco

Don Paul Albera, second successor of Don Bosco

Venerable Philip Rinaldi, third successor of Don Bosco

Venerable Mother Mary de Sales
Chappuis, the Visitation nun who
inspired the Oblate Foundations

Mother Frances de Sales Aviat,
foundress of the Oblate Sisters
of Saint Francis de Sales

Father Louis Brisson,
founder of the Oblates of
Saint Francis de Sales

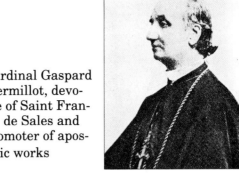

Cardinal Gaspard Mermillot, devotee of Saint Francis de Sales and promoter of apostolic works

Father Pierre Mermier, founder of the Missionaries of Saint Francis de Sales of Annecy

Saint Joseph Cafasso, spiritual director of Don Bosco

Co-founders of the Daughters of Saint Francis de Sales: *(left)* L'Abbé Henri Chaumont; *(top)* Venerable Caroline Colchen-Carré de Malberg

Bishop Louis Gaston de Ségur, founder of the Saint Francis de Sales Association for the Defense and Preservation of the Faith

The Circulation of the Writings
of Saint Francis de Sales

To infuse into the hearts of his young charges the thought
and image of the Salesian titular and patron as efficaciously
as possible, Don Bosco had sought initially to make his life
known by short biographies. One of these, perhaps only in a
limited edition, must have passed through the hands of the
boys of the oratory, including that of young Dominic Savio
(1842-1857), who used it for spiritual reading. Knowledge of
de Sales would have been assured through his major writings, of course, such as the *Introduction to the Devout Life*
and his *Letters*, and by the ample exposition of his thoughts
by means of the famous *Maxims*. Besides this Don Bosco
himself had the intention of writing a life of the saint—a
work of modest proportions and easy to read—but he only
got so far as to write out a draft or outline. However, what
he personally was unable to do, he accomplished through
others who wrote the life of the saint and reproduced salient
passages from his writings. Some works were printed in
their entirety. According to Father Valentini, the following
books were published by Salesian presses during the lifetime of the founder: *The Spiritual Awakening* (1862), *The
Maxims and Teachings of Saint Francis de Sales* (1876), the
Introduction to the Devout Life (1833) and the *Treatise on the
Love of God* (1884). (P 93)

Don Bosco's sons heeded his invitation, and several of
them wrote excellent biographies. One of these was Father
Barberis, the first master of novices of the congregation:
"Don Bosco chose Saint Francis de Sales as the titular and
patron of his first church and of his congregation, as a model
for himself and his followers in the education of the young.
He wanted one of us to write his life. In fact, he entrusted
this task to me. I followed the outline which he himself had
suggested. His aim was to put de Sales forward as the model
of a Christian life." (P 94)

Note Father Barberis's remark that he followed Don
Bosco's own outline of the life of the saint; this would have
been impossible if he did not have a good knowledge of it. In
any case, he clearly wanted the life of the Salesian patron

written, with the intention of making the thought and teachings of this great Doctor of the Church more widely known. He was convinced that one or more books of this kind, if simply written, would be of great help to young people.

To give this project importance he wanted the matter discussed in the superior chapter and even in the general chapters. Hence a more ambitious project was envisaged: to print and circulate the complete works of the saint.

The *Biographical Memoirs* reports on this ambitious enterprise:

> There was also need to make known the life and works of Saint Francis de Sales. There were biographies already in existence, but they did not seem suited to the young and to the times. Don Bosco, therefore, in January 1876 publicly invited the more outstanding Salesians to compile two lives of the saint: a short one, in one volume, suitable for the general public and the young, to be stocked in schools and parishes; the other, in two medium-size volumes, whose contents were to be gleaned from the most reliable authors and carefully written for educated people. He felt that whatever would help strengthen the Catholic teachings in face of Protestant principles ought to be extracted from the teachings of that saint and put into action. Once the life of Saint Francis de Sales was in print, he planned to publish a handy edition of his works as well. In the meantime he was eager for an early printing of the saint's *Philothea (Introduction)* in an attractive format, edited "for young people and educational institutions." Of course he wished that the complete works be published without abridgment. Publishing the complete works of Saint Francis de Sales in Italian was a daring project, and it reveals ever more how grand our founder's concepts were . . . (BM XI, 410)

He was even thinking about reprinting the Bollandists. His first Salesians, however, were aghast at these mind-boggling editorial ventures, and nothing was ever done about either project. Even more disappointing is the fact that future attempts, animated by the highest motives, were unsuccessful. Don Barberis did get Don Beltrami to translate into Italian the first few volumes of the critical edition of Saint Francis de Sales's works which was being produced at Annecy in 1892. These translations are still to be found in the central archives of the Salesian Congregation. Certainly not everyone could be expected to have the same courage or long-range views as the saint, nor should we take for granted that this project ought to have gone ahead no matter what the cost. Yet it is sad that such a wonderful initiative came to naught; there would have been a complete Italian translation based on the critical Annecy edition. What an eloquent testimony of Don Bosco's devotion to Saint Francis de Sales!

11

Don Bosco's Projects in Honor of Saint Francis de Sales

Declaration of Saint Francis de Sales as Doctor of the Church

In various ways and on many occasions Don Bosco sought publicly to express his veneration for the saint who was the titular and protector of his congregation. A good opportunity came in 1877 when Pope Pius IX proclaimed Saint Francis de Sales a Doctor of the Universal Church.

The times were difficult and hardly reassuring for Don Bosco; all sorts of misunderstandings and arguments with ecclesiastical authorities had arisen. He was facing difficulties, in particular, with Archbishop Gastaldi of Turin, who had turned against him and his congregation. This did not prevent Don Bosco from giving instructions to all his houses to celebrate the extraordinary event.

At the oratory in Valdocco, in the Basilica of Mary Help of Christians, every effort was made to share the universal joy. Don Bosco proceeded with great moderation, however, in order not to compete with or overshadow his bishop, who was directly involved in the official Turinese celebrations in honor of the Savoyard saint. He used the occasion of the first annual conference of the Cooperators in Rome, which was held in the hospitable and famous Tor de' Specchi in January 1878, to commemorate Saint Francis's being declared a Doctor. He arranged for the meeting to take place there because this institute had been the first in the city of Rome to sponsor help for boys in Salesian schools. (cf. *Salesian Bulletin*, January 1878)

Here is another interesting fact: the saintly bishop of Geneva stopped at Tor de' Specchi for a visit of devotion in March 1599. He had a special purpose for that trip, his only visit to the capital. On March 9, the feast of Saint Frances of Rome, he wanted to celebrate Mass in her honor, and it was here—he assures us of this himself—that he had the inspiration to found an institute like that of the Convent of Tor de' Specchi. After an interval of almost three hundred years, another saint, Don Bosco, came to the same locality with similar lofty intentions and spiritual projects in mind.

Don Bosco urged all to honor Saint Francis de Sales on this occasion as solemnly as possible. He appealed to the members of the Salesian family to take note of this great event. The *Salesian Bulletin*, quoting his words, movingly echoed the joy of the whole Church:

> It is a wonderful thing for us to let our Cooperators know that our patron, Saint Francis de Sales, was further glorified last year. Because of his great sanctity and learning, by his many writings, free from any taint of error, abounding in solid doctrine and inspiring great depths of piety, he was proclaimed by Pope Pius IX a Doctor of the Universal Church with the decree *Urbis et Orbis* on July 19, 1877. This new honor bestowed on him by the Holy See provides the motive to celebrate his feast more devoutly this year. If this cannot be done in public, at least all should celebrate it privately, in such a way that we know will be pleasing to our saint and to the greatest advantage to our souls. When the Cooperators are numerous enough they could arrange to have a sung Mass in their own parishes. In our house at Turin the feast will be celebrated with great solemnity and music specially chosen for the occasion. We will pray especially on that day that our patron will obtain for us the beautiful grace to treat our neighbors gently both in the way we speak with them and how we treat them. In that way, like Saint Francis, we will win over all hearts to God, especially those of poor youth. As true disciples of de Sales let our motto be: "Charity and gentle kindness." (*Salesian Bulletin*, January 1878)

This last exhortation reveals the spiritual attitude which was deeply imbedded in Don Bosco's devotion: that imitation is the most necessary virtue. By proposing this imitation he was going back many years to the resolution taken on the occasion of his first Mass: "The charity and gentleness of Saint Francis de Sales are to be my guide." (BM I, 385) He was determined to be faithful to this resolution until the end, especially when things were going badly, as in his tense relations with Archbishop Gastaldi. Under these difficult circumstances he had to set the example, exhort others to do the same, and encourage his followers to be patient.

Erection of an Altar at Annecy

In the process of maturing reflection on his holy patron, Don Bosco decided that as a final homage he would leave behind a lasting memorial which would record his own veneration for the saint as well as that of his entire congregation. A shrine was being built in the city of Annecy, close to the cradle of the Visitation. In May 1879, a request came from the convent of Annecy. We read of this in the *Biographical Memoirs*:

> When Saint Francis de Sales was proclaimed a Doctor of the Church in 1877, the Visitation nuns of Annecy set about to build a handsome shrine so that the sacred remains of their founder, enshrined until then in their convent, would find a resting place more honorable and more easily accessible to the public. Work on the shrine began in 1878. A year later, when the shrine's interior decorations still waited to be done, the funds had dwindled down to almost nothing. In May 1879, Don Bosco received a letter from Mother Mary Louise Bartolezzi, the superior, who wished to have his name memorialized in the new church. Turin had sent her a good number of donations in marble, granite, statues and other works of art, and it seemed natural for the shrine to contain also a tribute from the priest who had chosen Geneva's bishop as his congregation's patron saint. (BM XIV, 261-263)

Don Bosco was asked to sponsor an altar honoring the Sacred Heart of Jesus. Prompt and positive was his answer. "It is truly my heartfelt wish that our congregation, placed under the protection of this amiable saint, may erect an altar in your shrine as a token of our devotion . . ." (BM XIV, 262)

Amid many other preoccupations, none of them easily solved (among the difficulties was the fact that he had no money!), that famous altar was eventually erected, bearing this inscription in Latin: "The Salesian Congregation with the help of a Piedmontese gentleman, Feliciano Ricci des Ferres, decorated this chapel in the year 1880." Don Bosco had put the details into the hands of Count Cays, a Salesian, who in turn was able to find financial backing in the person of a zealous Cooperator.

Naturally one would have thought that the altar should be and remain a memorial, but both the church and the altar had a short life. In 1910, by a binding and irrevocable decision of the municipal council of Annecy, it was destroyed in a systematic town planning project which, as generally happens in these enterprises, did not concern itself very much with the rights of property owners, let alone shrines to saints. However, there still remains in Don Bosco's congregation an everlasting regard for this saint who continues to protect all who bear his venerated name.

Pilgrimage in Honor of the Saint

It is well known that Don Bosco traveled a good deal, or rather that he found it necessary to do so. Notwithstanding his many projects and commitments, which kept increasing following the erection and consolidation of his congregation, he had to go to Rome about twenty times in all. He was a guest in many of the cities of Italy and also traveled abroad. He went to Vienna several times to meet Count de Chambord, and to Barcelona, but the country he visited most frequently was France. However, he never had the opportunity, even as a pilgrim, to visit the various Salesian sacred places—those associated with the life of the Savoyard bishop. Yet there was one shrine in Paris he had to visit, both to satisfy his devotion and to pay his respects. This was Church of Saint Thomas of Villanova, where a statue of the Black Madonna was preserved. The young student Francis de Sales, praying fervently before this statue, was miraculously freed from the crisis of a temptation to despair of his eternal salvation. (cf. MB XVI, 185-186)

Don Bosco left a brief documentation as a memento of his visit on April 29, 1883. In the register for Masses, he wrote in French: "Father John Bosco, superior of the Pious Salesian Society, entrusts to Saint Francis de Sales all those works of which Saint Francis is the patron." (MB XVI, 186)

Among the works which the apostle of youth had at heart, one of the most important and pressing was that of safeguarding the many young people exposed to a whole barrage of corruption and seduction. With the help of Mary, more than ever looked upon as Our Lady of Perpetual Help, he would be able to win terrible spiritual battles. Following the example of Saint Francis de Sales, the young people had recourse to the maternal intercession of the holy virgin, invoking her just as the young student at Paris had done in that moment of crisis and spiritual upheaval. The episode was often recalled by Don Bosco in the form of an exhortation. It will help to refer to a description given by Ravier, an outstanding historian and biographer of Saint Francis de Sales:

> When he was a student at Paris, the saint fell prey to turbulent temptations and mental anguish; he was convinced that he was to be eternally damned, and he had no possible chance of salvation . . . One day it pleased divine providence to free him. While he was returning from the palace, passing in front of a church (Saint Stephen of the Greeks), he entered to pray. He placed himself in front of the statue of our Lady, where he found a prayer on a card on the kneeler: "Remember, O glorious Virgin Mary, that never has anyone implored your aid in vain . . ." He recited the whole prayer; then he stood up, and at that very moment he felt completely and totally cured. He felt that his temptation had fallen off him like the scales from the flesh of a leper.[16] (P 102)

Don Bosco treasured this prayer—attributed to Saint Bernard—all his life and had it included as an act of devotion in his *Companion of Youth*, noting that it was a strong weapon for every soul in need of freedom from temptation and sin.

At the Sacred Heart Basilica in Rome

If the memorial at Annecy was not to last, another witness of Don Bosco's love for this saint still remains in the Church of the Sacred Heart at Castro Pretorio in Rome, the construction of which had given poor Don Bosco so many headaches.

The altar and chapel in honor of the Salesian patron were built with the help of divine providence, often so unexpected and even miraculous, and with the help of generous donors. This project was close to Don Bosco's heart, for he dearly wanted to give a sign of his homage and veneration, as we can see from a brief talk he had with the cardinal vicar, the kindly protector of the Salesian Society:

> "In your Church of the Sacred Heart you will have a chapel dedicated to Saint Francis de Sales, your patron, will you not?"
> "Precisely, Your Eminence."
> "Good. I want to pay for the altar, and I hope that the protector of the congregation will give me the necessary enlightenment in the problems and annoyances reserved to the earthly protector of this pious society." (MB XVIII, 338-339)

Having described the chapel, the biographer points out some details concerning other representations of the saintly bishop of Geneva, depicted in various ways in the church. The facade is in travertine and decorated with statues, in marble and well-made; one of them is that of the holy patron, as is one of the mosaics inside the chapel. In the cupola, among the pictorial decorations, is Saint Margaret Mary Alacoque, a humble member of the Visitation Sisters and a spiritual daughter of Saint Francis. She stands amid a group of saints to whom our Divine Savior shows his heart all aflame. Saint Francis de Sales is also there, in a posture of contemplation, while some angels present him with the books he has written. Finally, there is the altar richly adorned.

We must not pass over some fine references from various sources and with diverse intents. On the occasion of the consecration of the basilica, the liberal newspaper *Fanfulla* wrote on May 15, 1887: "The great enlightened spirit of Saint Francis de Sales would have rejoiced over this great work, constructed on earth and giving evidence of boundless charity of soul . . ."

In the newspaper *The Citizen of Brescia*, there was an article entitled "The Works of Don Bosco" by the celebrated

Countess Lara, a pseudonym of the poetess Evelyn Cattermole Mancini:

This church arouses in all who visit it a profound feeling of emotion, when you think that it is still another miracle of a man who is the living image of Francis de Sales in this century. This humble priest succeeds in everything that he does because of his powerful intercession before God. All he does is blessed by heaven. Don Bosco is one of those privileged souls who from nothing brings into being so many enterprises. Even now one can foresee that one day, God knows when, his head will be encircled with a shining, golden light, the halo of the saints. (MB XVIII, 337-338)

As he reached the twilight of his life—just a few months before his death—Don Bosco was able to fix his gaze on the painting of his patron saint in this Basilica of the Sacred Heart. Many years earlier, before his oratory was established, he had looked at another portrait of the same saint, displayed in the porch of the institute of the marchioness Barolo in Turin. The image of this saint had cast its light on his whole life and was to remain bright in his vision even as his physical sight dimmed with the imminent approach of death.

12
Patron in Death

Let us return to Don Bosco's dream of May 9, 1879, which was mentioned briefly in chapter one. This was a rather long dream which would take several pages to recount in full. It told of a fierce battle between good and evil and the consequent need of vocations from among the young allies to Mary Help of Christians—future Salesians—who would spread to the north, south, east and west. Don Bosco relates:

Shortly afterward I witnessed a shower of flashing, fiery tongues of many colors, followed by thunder and then clear skies. Then I found myself in a charming garden. A man who looked like Saint Francis de Sales silently handed me a booklet. I asked him who he was. "Read the book," was the reply . . .

"Who are you?" I again asked the man who serenely gazed at me.

"Good people everywhere know me. I have been sent to tell you of future events."

"What are they?"

"Those you have already seen and those which you will ask about."

. . . Just then four men showed up bearing a coffin and approaching me.

"Whom is that for?" I asked.

"For you."

"How soon?"

"Do not ask. Just remember that you are mortal."

"What are you trying to tell me with this coffin?"

"That while you are still living you must see to it that your sons practice what they must continue to practice after your death. This is the heritage, the testament you must bequeath to them; but you must work on it and leave it [to your sons] as a well-studied and well-tested legacy."

"Can we expect roses or thorns?"

"Many roses and joys are in store, but very sharp thorns also threaten. They will cause all of you acute distress and sorrow. You must pray much."

"Should we open houses in Rome?"

"Yes, but not hurriedly; proceed with extreme prudence and caution."

"Is the end of my mortal life near at hand?"

"Don't be concerned. You have the rules and other books. Practice what you preach and be vigilant." (BM XIV, 88-90)

Preparation for Death

Though this dream took place some eight years before Don Bosco's death, it was a fair warning, for the saint's health gradually deteriorated until the end. Saint Francis de Sales apparently came in the dream, not only to be Don Bosco's teacher in a number of things, but also to be a harbinger of his death.

The end came in the early hours of January 31, 1888, scarcely a day after the feast of Saint Francis de Sales (celebrated at that time on January 29). It was as if his lifelong patron came looking for him. Don Bosco had lived out his life in the exaltation of the virtues of his favorite saint and had remained devoted to him to the last. All through his life, he had kept the saint's figure uppermost in his mind, and now his patron was returning that attention.

Let us recall some particular events of historical importance which occurred during Don Bosco's final two months. There is a beautiful reference to his patron as regards the future activities and mission of his sons, which took place after the feast of the Immaculate Conception in 1887, the last celebrated on earth by Don Bosco. On the morning of December 9, the founder said to Father Viglietti:

> The literal words of the immaculate virgin, who appeared to me last night, were: "It is pleasing to God and the Blessed Virgin that the sons of Saint Francis de Sales open a house at Liege in honor of the Blessed Sacrament. Here the glories of God will be manifested publicly and from here we must spread that glory into all the families connected with you and especially among the many young people who, in many parts of the world, are or who will be confided to their care." (MB XVIII, 438)

After a brief period of confinement to his bed, Don Bosco recovered somewhat in the second week of December, unexpectedly and contrary to the predictions of the doctors. The return to reasonably good health amazed even the patient himself. This recovery lasted for the better part of the month of January, about twenty days in all. It seemed like a new lease on life, almost as if he were enjoying a second birth. He remarked to his secretary: "Viglietti, see that you ask Don Lemoyne how he can explain how a person, after twenty days in bed, with his mind weakened in the extreme . . . can suddenly recover to such an extent that he can understand everything, and feel strong enough to get up, to write, to work . . . as healthy as if he had never been sick." The saint then offered his own explanation, saying that what God can do by His own power, Mary obtained by her intercession. (ibid., 512)

It is not presumptuous to think that Don Bosco's patron was also watching over him with delicate care, protecting him and, as it were, accompanying him as he was about to take the final step. No doubt he was especially at his side at that supreme time of his life. There are a few striking coincidences worthy of consideration. One of these occurred at the beginning of the novena to Saint Francis de Sales, and the other took place on the very feast of the titular.

On January 20 Don Bosco had a visit from Bishop Philip Francesco, titular bishop of Lara, of the Salesian Congregation of Annecy, coadjutor of Bishop Tissot of the same Congregation of Missionaries of Saint Francis de Sales. (cf. MB XVIII, 526) Was this, too, a gesture on the part of Saint Francis de Sales, who had lived so many years at Annecy? Certainly it was the fulfillment of a wish of a representative of that See to visit a man whose fame had spread as another Francis de Sales on earth.

In any case it was from this time that those around Don Bosco realized that the end was very near. His biographer relates: "The worsening of the illness, dating from January 20, the first day of the novena to Saint Francis de Sales, went on gradually until the feast of the holy patron, on which day the venerable invalid became paralyzed and lost the use of his speech." (ibid., 539)

As the situation deteriorated, a beautiful and unforgettable event occurred. Twelve youngsters, headed by Don Bosco's secretary, made an offering of their own lives, all signing this prayer: "O Jesus in the Blessed Sacrament, Mary Help of Christians, Saint Francis de Sales our patron, we the undersigned offer our lives in exchange for the life of our beloved Don Bosco. Deign to accept our offering." (ibid.) This prayer was placed under the corporal during a Mass celebrated for Don Bosco by Don Berto and served by Aloysius Orione, one of the signers.[17]

On the day of the feast of Saint Francis de Sales, January 29, Don Bosco was able to receive communion for the last time. "When the priest came to give him the sacred Host, Don Bosco was dozing . . . but as soon as Don Viglietti said in a loud voice, *Corpus Domini Nostri Jesu Christi*, the invalid woke up, opened his eyes, joined his hands and, having made his communion, remained recollected, repeating the words of thanksgiving suggested to him by Don Sala. This was Don Bosco's final communion." (MB XVIII, 535) Soon after this he again became delirious.

An indication leads us to suppose that he had a presentiment that his mental deterioration would begin from that day. When Don Rua asked him on the second day he was in bed, as his rector and confessor, for a renewal of his dispensation from saying the breviary, Don Bosco had replied: "I will grant you that until the feast of Saint Francis de Sales. After that, if you still need it, get Don Lemoyne to renew it." (MB XVIII, 535-536)

Events continue to surprise us. Certain lucid moments allowed Don Bosco to be fully aware of anything of importance happening at the time or when his response was required.

We have used the word "delirious," but his declining strength did not rob him entirely of the lucidity of his mind. In fact about 10 A.M., with full awareness, he asked Don Durando the time, what was happening in the church, what feast they were celebrating, and recalling that it was the feast of Saint Francis de Sales, he showed his pleasure . . . That evening (29) he could still recognize and bless Count Incisa, the prior of the feast of Saint Francis de Sales, and the bishop of Susa, Bishop Rosaz, who preached the panegyric of the saint. (MB XVIII, 536)

All had the impression that the holy patron—on the day of his liturgical glorification—wanted to stand by his devotee forever, so that he might have joy without end. His biographer notes the singular coincidences of this solemnity:

The day of the feast of Saint Francis de Sales dawned. There was the ringing of the bells, singing, pontificating; but in the hearts of all there was sadness. It can even be said that the sacred rite announced an imminent mourning. During the Mass the second letter of Paul to Timothy was read:

I for my part am already being poured out like a libation. The time of my dissolution is near. I have fought the good fight, I have finished the race, I have kept the faith. From now on a merited crown awaits me; on that Day the Lord, just judge that he is, will award it to me—and not only to me, but to all who have looked for his appearing with eager longing. (2 Tm 4:6-8)

While the subdeacon sang those words, many heads were bowed; tears flowed down many cheeks; it seemed as if the voice of the Lord was saying: Don Bosco's pilgrimage is over. (MB XVIII, 535)

That pilgrimage did come to a close on January 29, even if death did not come to take him until the early morning of January 31.

In his continual state of drowsiness he was not aware of anything, except when someone spoke to him of paradise or things of the soul. At those times he bowed his head. Even on some days he often repeated: "Mother, Mother!"—sometimes adding: "Tomorrow, tomorrow; Jesus, Jesus, Mary . . . Mary! Jesus and Mary, I give you my heart and my soul." (MB XVIII, 536-537)

At 4:30 A.M. [January 31] the bells of Mary Help of Christians rang out the Ave Maria, and all quietly said the Angelus . . . [The saint] gave three sighs at brief intervals . . . "Don Bosco is really dead," exclaimed Don Belmonte. (ibid.)

Don Bosco had ended his earthly days with a vivid memory of, and at the same time very deep homage to, the saint whom he had loved and invoked for most of his life. He was Salesian right up to his final moments, with the holy ambition to be with him—heart to heart—in the grand temple of eternity.

After Death: the Two Saints Reunited in Glory

Even after Don Bosco's death we come face-to-face with something amazing—it may even seem incredible! Let us look at the incident as told in the *Biographical Memoirs*:

The clock on the bell tower of the internal church of Saint Francis de Sales had not been going since 1865, and the hands stood still at 4:20 for many years. Don Lemoyne had taken note of this time, thinking that they could have some relation with the hour in which the activities of Don Bosco would be terminated by death. Seven years later the hands of the clock were moved because some boys, climbing up the tower, had moved the hands for fun. Don Lemoyne, however, with that idea in his head, went to have a look at the clock the morning Don Bosco died. To his amazement he saw that after so many years after the hands had been moved they had returned to the original 4:20. (MB XVIII, 542)

So even the silent hands of the clock of the bell tower—in the very church where the body of Don Bosco was to lie in repose for the solemn funeral honors—spoke over a long period, well before his death, and gave an indication of a fateful time, calculated to the hour, so full of meaning!

These two saints—Francis de Sales and John Bosco—in life had *felt* alike, *spoke* alike and *thought* alike. Now they were finally united in a spiritual embrace. On earth, the *heart* of the first had been preserved as a very precious relic in the Visitation Convent at Treviso. Not far away, the *brain* and *tongue* of the other were to remain miraculously intact in the Basilica of Mary Help of Christians in Turin. Did God have a purpose in preserving these remains of the two saints as a sign for us and for future generations? In any case we can draw inspiration from the Salesian spirit that flowed from them, the shining example of their lives and the precious legacy they left through the instrumentality of tongue, brain and heart.

The two saints are also reunited, one may say, in their outward glorification. In the Basilica of Saint Peter in the Vatican, a short distance one from the other—almost pointing to each other—they stand in niches reserved for founders of orders and congregations. They are close to the altar of the confessional and above the statue of Saint Peter. From this perspective they seem to convey an ideal message: to spread throughout the entire world, to everyone everywhere, the Salesian spirit.

Saint Francis de Sales and Don Bosco were both intrepid champions of God, raised up to defend and sustain the truths of faith, especially the primacy of Peter. They exemplify fidelity to the Church and indefectible attachment to the teaching authority of the pope. They represent a common and perennial message from the center of Christianity, which we receive in a spirit of humble submission. Their teaching fills our hearts with joy and urges us to imitate the love that they proclaimed by their lives.

13

Devotion of Don Bosco's Successors to Saint Francis de Sales

Quite often in his writings, Don Bosco took the opportunity of referring to the thought and spirit of his holy protector, as for example in the *Catholic Readings* or the *Companion of Youth*. More particularly, he did so in that book which is a quasi autobiography, the *Memoirs of the Oratory of Saint Francis de Sales*. Even a simple reading leaves the clear impression that it was the Holy Spirit who gave him "the apostolic zeal and goodness of heart of Saint Francis de Sales." (*Acts of the Salesian Special General Chapter*, 10, 142)

Don Bosco's sons, following so noble an example and teaching, fortunately were able to imbibe that spirit proper to de Sales, and they also knew how to hand it down unadulterated to future generations. In particular, his first three successors made excellent use of the riches of this tradition and passed on this treasure. Drawing on their firsthand experience, they enriched it with their own devotion and attitudes, making full use of his writings in their circular letters, which abound in Salesian quotations. This phenomenon of a singular and devout dependence was stressed and clarified in a very special way on the occasion of the great Salesian event, the third centenary of the death of the holy bishop of Geneva (1922). Today one has only to take up these circulars and reread them to see how faithful they are to Salesian tradition. They transmit in a fatherly way all the precious ascetical and religious patrimony of the saint.

Of course these successors had at hand the many lives of the saint that were in print at the time in countless editions. There were as well numerous collections of *Maxims*, which were gold mines of Francis's favorite sayings. We must not expect to find the source of every quotation given, nor that the quotation agrees in every detail with the original, nor that it was taken directly from an original source. In those days this strict methodology was not demanded, as it would be today.

Don Michael Rua

Father Rua was accustomed to call Saint Francis de Sales "our own glorious patron," "holy doctor," "the most gentle and kindly Saint Francis de Sales." (cf. *Lettere circolari di Don Michael Rua*, 399, 415, 434) We also have the testimony of Father Joseph Vespignani concerning a practice during the year 1876-1877 that must have been inspired, or perhaps suggested by, the founder: "Don Rua's office was a place of piety and prayer. As soon as you entered, he devoutly recited the *Actiones* and a Hail Mary, and then read out a brief thought from the writings of Saint Francis de Sales; he ended the day's work the same way; namely, with the reading of a maxim from our saint, followed by the *Agimus* and a Hail Mary." (P 144)

Father Rua evidently had a fair degree of familiarity with the doctrine of de Sales. He was able to quote him in matters ascetical, especially as regards spiritual direction and Holy Communion: "If you want to walk safely along the road to salvation—says Saint Francis de Sales—find someone who can give you spiritual direction. (cf. O III, 22) My God, how happy I would be if one day after communion I should find my heart outside my breast, and in its place the heart of Christ." (cf. O XV, 51)

It was especially at the beginning of the century, on the occasion of the consecration of the Salesian Society to the Sacred Heart of Jesus, that Don Rua waxed eloquent in his esteem for Saint Francis de Sales, the "Doctor of the Devotion to the Sacred Heart," extolling the saint's own love for the divine heart and quoting from his works. (cf. *Lettere circolari di Don Michael Rua*, November 20, 1900)

Don Paul Albera

Don Paul Albera declared that Don Bosco was a disciple of Saint Francis de Sales because he had so faithfully followed the teachings given by the saint in the *Introduction to the Devout Life*. In this regard Father Ricaldone has written in his treatise, *La Pietà:* "According to Don Bosco's second successor, it was in order to more securely follow in the footsteps of his divine Master that Don Bosco was attracted to the doctrine of the gentle Saint Francis de Sales. Hence, later on, he chose him as the patron of his work." (P 145-147)

In his own circular letters Don Albera has written:

Reading with devotion the biographies of Saint Francis de Sales, written both by his contemporaries and by modern authors, we realize that they are permeated by a supernatural pedagogy. At the same time we are strongly reminded of another life [Don Bosco's] which we, for the most part, saw lived out before our very eyes. The educational principles in the two lives are the same: love, gentleness, familiarity, a heart filled with the holy fear of God, the forestalling and prevention of evil so as not to have need of recourse to punishments. (L 553-554)

On these subjects Don Albera had occasion to develop his thoughts at length through his edifying letters. Father Ricaldone cites various references to Saint Francis de Sales that Father Albera found inspiring:

Speaking of God

When will that day come when we, according to the lively expression of Saint Francis de Sales, let ourselves be carried like our Lord as a child in the arms of his mother?

In Relation to Faith

Let us recall to mind the sentiments of gratitude of our own Saint Francis de Sales as he exclaims: "My God, how great and numerous are your gifts for which I must be grateful. But how can I thank Him for having giving me the gift of faith? When I contemplate the immensity of this gift I feel like dying of love."

As Regards the Lord's Graces

Saint Francis de Sales used to say that favors showered down from the hand of God upon us are thicker than the snow which fell upon the mountains of his Savoy.

Concerning Obedience

Obedience would be very dear to us if we reflected with Saint Francis de Sales that this virtue is like the salt that gives taste and flavor to all our actions . . . The Salesian knows that it is his duty to be a humble instrument in the hands of his superiors; his way of acting is constantly practiced according to the maxim of our protector: Ask for nothing, refuse nothing.

As Regards Corrections

It is hoped that there should be great calm both in the one who gives the corrections and in the one who receives them, so that the correction will both profit the one and the other. This is what Saint Francis de Sales taught, and this is the way dear Don Bosco acted.

As Regards Charity

Let us follow the example of Saint Francis de Sales, who said that he made a pact with his tongue never to speak when his heart was not at peace. (Ricaldone, Don Peter. *La Pietà*, 268-270)

Let us now examine some sources—used by Don Albera on various occasions—that come from Francis de Sales:

True Devotion

Souls which are really pious (in the de Sales text, "men who have angelic hearts") have wings to allow them to fly to God in prayer and have feet to walk among men by means of a humble and holy life. (O III, 18)

Divine and Heavenly Friendship

No company, no occupation should impede us from being with Jesus, Mary, with the angels and with the saints. (O XIII, 321)

Devotion to Mary

I know full well what a great fortune it is to be a son, even though unworthy, of such a glorious mother. Trusting in her protection, let us put our hands to great enterprises; if the soul burns with ardent affection, we will obtain whatsoever we need. (O XV, 258; a letter to Mother Chantal, August 15, 1612.)

The Practice of Chastity

Chastity is the lily of the virtues: it raises man to the level of angels . . . (O III, 175) So Francis de Sales writes with good reason that chastity is a timid virtue, even suspicious and fainthearted; a single word is enough to alarm it, a look to frighten it.

Self-Control

He who is not able to conquer his repugnances becomes ever weaker and weaker. (O XVII, 341; a letter to a religious.)

Don Philip Rinaldi

The Salesian tradition of devotion to the saintly patron continued with the third successor of Don Bosco. The venerable servant of God was accustomed to present Don Bosco "as one of the most splendid personifications of charity in our times," a replica of the great bishop of Geneva who, in his turn, was described as "an outstanding educator in the ways of perfection." (*Circular Letters of Don Philip Rinaldi. ASC,* 1924, 175)[18]

The invitation to solemnize the centenary in honor of de Sales was first made by Don Albera but was realized and successfully brought to a conclusion by Don Rinaldi, giving an impetus to a closer study of the works of the saint and a deeper knowledge of his doctrine and the dynamics of his apostolate. Don Rinaldi insisted that all Salesians should continue this study, recommending especially the work that had just come from the pen of Don Ceria on the religious life as presented in the teachings of Saint Francis de Sales. He concluded his letter by reminding the confreres of the dream, previously mentioned, which Don Bosco had on May 9, 1879, in which "a man who looked like Saint Francis de Sales" appeared to him and gave him some wise observations and practical advice.

Referring in passing to Don Bosco's love for knowledge, Don Rinaldi observed that even in this he had Francis as his model. He desired to inculcate the same attitude in his Salesians, especially the priests: "Don Bosco showed in his own life how much he esteemed study, even to the point of heroic sacrifice. For this reason, too, he gave us as our protector Saint Francis de Sales, the holy doctor, who declared that study is, for the priest, the eighth sacrament." (ibid.) The original statement of Saint Francis de Sales was: "The learning of the priest is the eighth sacrament of the Church. The greatest disasters have occurred when this learning is in the hands of others but not in those of the levites." (O XXIII, 303-304)

Don Rinaldi put Saint Francis de Sales forward as an exemplar of sanctity, and in this he was following in the footsteps of the founder. He said in a conference to an early group of the Volunteers of Don Bosco: "Don Bosco began his work under the influence of Saint Francis de Sales . . . He understood that Saint Francis de Sales must be his model; even though their work was different, they still lived in practice the same spirit of gentleness, meekness and zeal for the defense of the faith." (Conference to the Zelatrici di

Maria Ausiliatrice, who later took the name of Volunteers of Don Bosco, December 30, 1920.)

In a previous conference to the same group, he had insisted upon meekness, the preeminent characteristic of the bishop of Geneva. "Ask the Holy Spirit to enlighten you at the beginning of this new year [1920]. Bear in mind the meekness of the child Jesus, and do not forget that this is the month of Saint Francis de Sales, the master of humility and meekness." (P 149)

In the solemn celebrations for the golden jubilee of the *Salesian Constitutions*, he wrote: "Here another reflection comes spontaneously to mind. To honor our heavenly patron in the third centenary of his death, we sought to study his writings. We wanted to understand the characteristics of his moral figure and the spirit which inspired our society. This study has awakened in us the desire to discover the same spirit in the writings of our father and of his immediate successors, Don Rua and Don Albera." (*Circular Letters of Don Philip Rinaldi*. ASC 1924, 175)

Father Rinaldi issued several invitations to celebrate with devotion the annual feast of Saint Francis de Sales. Often his request ended with a fervent prayer:

> Saint Francis de Sales is an outstanding educator in the way of perfection, and his works are totally permeated by that pedagogy which our founder took up several centuries later, adapting them with so much art. He achieved this, not on paper, but in the society created by him for the salvation of youth, baptized by him with the name of Salesian precisely to indicate to the future members the source from which he drew from time to time, so as to ensure an abundant and vital supply.
>
> May Saint Francis de Sales, our glorious patron, obtain for us from the Lord that there may reign among us the spirit of his kindness and peace which is the spirit handed on to us by our father Don Bosco in the *Constitutions*, and which he had practiced so gently and so constantly . . . May our good father help us to live according to this spirit in every one of our houses, inspiring in our hearts love and devotion. For according to Saint Francis de Sales it is love that lightens our fatigue and gives joy to our life. It causes us to walk heartily and joyfully, with filial affection, in the performance of works pleasing to God our Father. At the same time, in this way, we lead many souls to Him

. . . May Saint Francis de Sales obtain for us the grace to become his true followers. (ibid., 1923 and 1924)

Father Peter Ricaldone

Father Ricaldone strove to continue the tradition handed down by the first three successors of Don Bosco; his writings bear witness to this fact. In his work, *La Pietà,* he referred to the prayer to Saint Francis de Sales, which was recited every day as a constant homage of Salesian devotion and gratitude to the patron. He went on to express a fear that as a consequence of the canonization of Don Bosco an erroneous opinion might take root. Given the proximity of the two liturgical feasts of Saint Francis de Sales and Saint Don Bosco (celebrated at that time on January 29 and January 31 respectively), devotion to Saint Francis de Sales might suffer. He continued:

All of us must fight against this danger, because it would be the cause of immense damage to the spirit of piety proper to the Salesian family of Don Bosco . . . So let us make every effort to imitate his piety, as well as his gentleness, his zeal for the salvation of souls, and his detachment from every human affection . . . An excellent way of showing our devotion to our patron and titular would be the reading of his marvelous writings, which so strongly encourage us to tend towards Christian holiness and religious perfection. The *Introduction,* the *Treatise on the Love of God,* his *Spiritual Letters* and his *Treatises* may form a delightful pasture for our souls . . . We Salesians, however, must not be content with carrying in our very name the clearest and most eloquent sign of our devotion to Saint Francis de Sales, but we must aim at making this devotion vital. (Ricaldone, Don Peter. *La Pietà,* 266, 267, 268, 272)

Shortly before his death in 1951 (ASC 164), Father Ricaldone published his circular letter on Don Bosco's devotion to the pope, finding in this attachment to the vicar of Christ a reminder of the same characteristic in Saint Francis de Sales.

To some extent the fear of Father Ricaldone mentioned above proved to be prophetic. After Don Bosco's canonization in 1934 and after Father's own death, there seemed to develop within the society a kind of eclipse of Saint Francis de Sales. For a few decades, when understandably devotion to the founder was at an all-time high, explicit devotion to the patron seemed to fade somewhat into the background.

Father Aloysius Ricceri

On the occasion of the third centenary of the death of Saint Francis de Sales (1967), Pope Paul VI issued an apostolic letter on the saint, *Subaudiae Gemma* (*The Gem of Savoy*). To commemorate this event, the sixth successor of Don Bosco, Father Ricceri, wrote:

> It is evident that Don Bosco was a convinced and diligent disciple of the bishop of Geneva, and it is also evident that this is the line the Church invites us to adopt in our preaching and discussions. I would add just this, that a little thought shows that what has been said reveals the essential elements in our own method of education. Dear confreres, not only in preaching, discussions, meetings with adults, but also in our relations with our boys, we must be always influenced by a spirit of understanding, gentleness and peace if we would obtain positive results in our contacts. Charity always wins.
>
> All of which suggests that today an ever-deeper knowledge of the doctrine and the spirit of our patron saint and of the method of education of Don Bosco is as necessary as ever it was. It is not a rare thing to find that the knowledge of this method which we ourselves have is only partial and empirical, and for this very reason we do not appreciate it adequately, and we interpret and use it in an arbitrary way. The results are painfully negative and sometimes nullify our work in education.
>
> Instead today—and here a word of encouragement—in places which seemed arid deserts, but where we have been called to work with very difficult boys, we have witnessed a heartwarming transformation obtained by the intelligent use and diligent practice of the Salesian method.

Father Egidio Viganò

The seventh successor of Don Bosco, Father Viganò, in his letter on Salesian devotion to Mary Help of Christians (1978), quoting Father Albera, described Don Bosco "as a disciple of our own Saint Francis de Sales" in respect to his great devotion to our Lady. Furthermore, in his letter on the Salesian family (1982), he pointed to the pastoral charity of

Don Bosco as the very heart of his charism and spirit, derived from the "ecstasy of action" taught by Saint Francis de Sales.

In conclusion, we can say that the successors of Don Bosco have linked Saint Francis de Sales to the principal aspects of the founder's spirituality, with its primacy of love: the devotion to the Sacred Heart and the Eucharist (Don Rua); devotion to Mary (Don Albera); vital prayer (Don Rinaldi); devotion to the pope (Father Ricaldone); the Preventive System (Father Ricceri); apostolic activity as ecstasy of action (Father Viganò).[19]

His successors realized full well that in promoting devotion to Saint Francis de Sales they were not alone. After Don Bosco's canonization, Pope Pius XI remarked, "Now Don Bosco belongs to the whole Church." The same could have been said about Saint Francis de Sales centuries earlier. For this reason, part four of this book will extol the cosmopolitan spirit of Saint Francis de Sales.

Parts II and III in Retrospect

In unpublished notes, Father John Ayers, SDB, offers the following considerations about the maturing years and aftermath, confirming the "spiritual consanguinity" between Don Bosco and Saint Francis de Sales.

The Same Spirit

As "the evening closed in," Don Bosco increasingly turned to Francis de Sales for the future well-being of his congregation. He sent a reminder to Bishop Lasagna or Bishop Costamagna in South America:

Imitate the gentleness of Saint Francis de Sales in speaking and acting with all classes of people . . . The Salesian system is uniquely ours; never blows, never harsh words.

Or a letter to rectors, or one on punishments (written on the patron's day, 1876):

Our dear, gentle patron Francis de Sales—educator of hearts—as you know had made a pact with his tongue never to speak while his heart was upset.

Such anxiety about a colder, institutional spirit in the expanding congregation was to climax with Don Bosco's famous letter from Rome (1884) on charity. This classical educational oratorio would come to its crescendo with this appeal:

Let us all agree on this then: may the charity of those who command and the charity of those who must obey cause the spirit of Saint Francis de Sales to reign among us.

Regular Occurrences and Recommendations

The annual feast of Saint Francis de Sales (then January 29) was kept as *the* Salesian feast, preceded by a novena, personal nosegays, special "Good Nights," voting on good conduct, etc., and climaxed with all the liturgical, theatrical and refectorial solemnity that the oratory could muster. "Are you preparing a splendid feast for our patron?" Don Bosco asked from Rome. He instructed Don Berto to open the chapel and the cellar for the occasion, choosing a kind benefactor to pay the bill and act as patron for the family feast, inviting him to preside over the evening's theater and prize-giving. This latter, involving both clerics and pupils, was a unique feature of the patronal day.

For Cooperators also the patronal feast was special. Somehow, Don Bosco always found time to give them lengthy conferences on that day (or close to it), while in their first regulations they were asked to assist at Mass on January 29 to gain a plenary indulgence on patron's day (just as Salesians would receive the indulgence by offering Mass for deceased parents on the day following).

The rectors' meeting on the patronal feast day evolved into the first general chapter. From 1865 onwards, every January 29 Don Bosco would call the rectors together for their annual reports about each house in Italy and France, followed by his special conference. The opening talk was very often on Francis de Sales and his spirit. Such meetings grew into the first official chapter in 1876. At this chapter Don Bosco expressly noted: "Saint Francis of Sales, our patron, will also preside over our meetings and will hopefully obtain the help we need from God to make our deliberations in keeping with his spirit." (BM XIII, 183)

Special Events

After Francis de Sales was declared a Doctor of the Church, Don Bosco sponsored the Sacred Heart altar in the new church dedicated to the saint in Annecy, although this is not the one that now stands. In 1887, when the Salesian Basilica of the Sacred Heart was consecrated in Rome, the officiating prelate, Cardinal Parocchi, the pope's vicar, insisted on donating the altar dedicated to Saint Francis de Sales.

Don Lemoyne tells how Don Bosco constantly promoted devotion to and imitation of his patron:

. . . when talking to his boys then, and later on as well, he would bring out some sayings or episodes of the saint's life. Above all he endeavored to portray to them the saint's gentleness, which had brought back to the Church so many heretics. (BM II, 197)

In 1883, Don Bosco wrote in the Mass register of Saint Thomas of Villanova Church in Paris (home of Francis's Black Madonna statue):

Father John Bosco, superior of the pious Salesian Society, recommends all his works to Saint Francis de Sales, their patron.

In several dream-visions, but notably the one in 1879, Francis de Sales appeared as a guide, a majestic personage of gentle appearance. He predicted to Don Bosco the future of the society and gave sound advice to the novices, the professed, the rectors and the superior. The congregation will last

. . . as long as its members love work and temperance. Should either of these two pillars fall, your entire edifice will collapse and crush superiors, subjects and followers beneath it. (BM XIV, 89)

There is enough internal evidence to suggest that the majestic person in priestly garments of the Ten Diamonds dream also represents Francis de Sales. In a wider sense it represents both Don Bosco and de Sales, whose spirits were the same.

After his great Mission Dream in 1883, Don Bosco told his Salesians that with the gentle kindness of Saint Francis de Sales they would attract to Jesus Christ the entire population of the Americas. This was almost a paraphrase of Francis's own words, that the whole world would accept the message of salvation if it were made attractive.

Spreading Knowledge and Devotion

Among the reading list of books suggested to pupils, Cooperators and others, Don Bosco always included his patron's works, especially the *Introduction to the Devout Life* and the *Treatise on the Love of God*. The first Salesian novice master under Don Bosco's tutelage, Father Barberis, constantly turned the novices' attention to Francis de Sales, insisting that the very first thing that a novice must acquire is the spirit proper to the congregation; namely, the spirit of Saint Francis de Sales. In his *Vademecum* for young Salesians he inserted the *Rule of Life* or directory that Saint Francis de Sales wrote as a student at Padua.

Having seen the need for good books and popular Christian literature, Don Bosco turned to Francis de Sales for inspiration as a popular preacher, writer and publisher in setting up his own printing press and trying his hand as an author in that secular, anticlerical age, equivalent to the Geneva of Francis's day.

For many years Don Bosco cherished the idea not only of publishing his patron's two classics (*Introduction* and *Treatise*) but also his *Omnia Opera*, Francis's complete life and works in a critical edition. Of even more significance was Don Bosco's often expressed desire to put out a popular edition of the *Introduction to the Devout Life*, so adapted as to be attractive to and suitable for the young. He personally supervised the publication of *Maxims of Saint Francis de Sales* in 1876, the *Philothea (Introduction to the Devout Life)* in 1883, and the *Theotimus (Treatise on the Love of God)* in 1884. He consigned the two-volume life to Don Barberis (1887-1888), while the *Opera Omnia* never got past the first two volumes (still in manuscript in the Salesian archives) translated by Don Beltrami.

Don Bosco looked to his Salesian houses as centers of devotion to Francis de Sales and as dynamos of Salesian spirituality:

For pupils: *When you go home for the holidays tomorrow, I want you to spread the gentle influence of Francis de Sales everywhere you go— among your families and friends, in your parishes and villages.*

For past pupils: *I am delighted to see here today at this reunion three of the original oratory boys. I regard as belonging to the Salesian family anyone who has come—even for a short time—under the gentle influence of Saint Francis de Sales . . . and has been educated with his maxims.*

For Cooperators: *The Cooperators help preserve and spread in the world the spirit of the Congregation of Saint Francis de Sales.*

This concept was taken up by Don Rinaldi (Don Bosco "Redivivus") when elected rector major in 1922: "Make the life, writings and spirit of Saint Francis de Sales known far and wide," he told the assembled Salesians.

Finally, there is Don Bosco's striking comparison of his Salesians' relationship with Francis de Sales to that of the Jesuits with Ignatius Loyola—almost a founding connection. He told his early followers that it was his keenest wish to see the congregation grow and its apostolic sons multiply. He expressed the hope that the members of his society would prove themselves to be zealous and worthy sons of Saint Francis de Sales, just as the Jesuits are faithful sons of the brave Saint Ignatius Loyola.

On January 29, 1888, the patron's feast, Don Bosco received communion for the last time.

Substantial as all this evidence is, it does not on its own constitute an overwhelming case for the "Salesian connection" unless it is set within its overall historical context. Of crucial significance here is the fact that whenever Don Bosco was confronted with a major decision, a historic moment or a crisis of decline, in his own life or in the life of the congregation, he turned without fail to the life, inspiration and spiritual teaching of Saint Francis de Sales. This was true at his ordination, at the oratory's start, at the congregation's birth, at the writing of the first rule, at the first general chapter, at the foundation of the Daughters of Mary Help of Christians, at the start of the South American mission, at crucial meetings with Cooperators and past pupils, in important dreams, in moments of Church-state conflict, at the breakdown of the Preventive System or of the religious family spirit, and so on.

There were very few times when Francis de Sales was *not* invoked as the authoritative, decisive weight to tip the precarious Salesian scales back to their equilibrium. (Significantly, Don Bosco could have just as easily invoked Canon Law or the society's *Constitutions*, but he did not.) How did he regard Francis de Sales, then? As model, patron, inspiration? Yes, all these certainly, but much more. For Don Bosco, Francis de Sales was the living library of Salesianity from whom he drew all his vital core principles of education and religious life, especially when cracks appeared at the margins. Francis was the Godfather of Salesian spirituality entrusted with the human and Christian development of this young, neophyte congregation dedicated to his name.

It seems fair enough to say—as hypothesis only—that in Don Bosco's eyes, the Salesian (past pupil, Cooperator, etc.) is the

Philothea of Saint Francis de Sales, with the *Introduction to the Devout Life* as the remote primer of the Preventive System. At a deeper level, the Salesian religious (SDB, FMA, VDB) is the patron's beloved Theotimus, with the *Treatise on the Love of God* as the original encyclopedia of Salesian spirituality.

Let all the followers of Saint Francis de Sales listen to the voice of experience as Don Bosco speaks of the success of his great Salesian project: "Anyone else, even today, could achieve just as much by emulating the simplicity and gentleness of Saint Francis de Sales." (BM III, 39)

PART IV

The Cosmopolitan Spirit of Saint Francis de Sales

14

The Nineteenth Century: the Salesian Century

The nineteenth century has been called the Salesian century because of the many manifestations of devotion to the saint of Savoy that sprang up in that era. The Holy Father, Pius IX, led the way in this devotion. Before becoming pope he had participated in a confraternity set up to honor the saint by a monthly meeting and by a daily private reading from his works. Even as pope he kept a holy picture of the saint on his desk and always had at his side the booklet entitled *Maxims of Saint Francis de Sales*. On the occasion of his episcopal jubilee (1877), he declared that Francis de Sales "belongs heart and soul to me . . . I also possess a fiber of the heart of this saint." He was referring to a gift of the Sisters of the Visitation at Venice. In the same year he proclaimed Saint Francis de Sales a Doctor of the Church.

Don Bosco recorded that the Holy Father suggested and wholeheartedly concurred in the decision to name the Salesian Society after Saint Francis de Sales. (See page 39.) As has been mentioned previously, in the Church of the nineteenth century there were many associations which took their name and inspiration from Francis de Sales, not only in Italy but in other parts of Europe as well. The same is true of the twentieth century, as we will see later.

Salesian Families

In the nineteenth century, several male religious congregations were founded that claim Saint Francis de Sales as their special patron. The most famous and largest is that of Saint John Bosco, but there are two others that merit our consideration.

The first is the Missionaries of Saint Francis de Sales (MSFS), who go by the name "Fransalians." They thrive today in India, where they have three provinces. The following is an excerpt adapted and updated from the *Catholic Encyclopedia* (original edition) explaining their origin:

> Amid the many activities to which Saint Francis de Sales devoted himself, he long had the desire to found a society of priests animated by his spirit. His desire became reality only after his death, when Raymond Bonal (1600-1653) founded the "Society of the Priests of the Visitation and of Saint Francis de Sales," but this society did not outlive the French Revolution. Two centuries later, Pierre-Joseph Rey, a successor of the saint in the See of Annecy, broached the subject of founding a similar society to Father Pierre-Marie Mermier (1790-1862), who had been considering the same idea. Father Mermier put the design into execution, and the institute was formed in 1830. The congregation was canonically instituted in 1838. The society was not to be a mere association of priests, but a new religious congregation, bound by simple vows. Hence Father Mermier, the first superior general, offered himself and his companions to the pope for foreign missions. In 1845 his offer was accepted by the Propaganda, and the first missionaries of Saint Francis de Sales set out for India. The work has prospered. The dioceses of Nazgpur and Vizagapatam have profited much by their missionary endeavors, and today they count many native vocations. The society has been established also in England and the United States.

Father Mermier also founded the Sisters of the Cross of Chavanod, in association with Claudine Echernier, to undertake missionary work, especially in India, in the spirit of Saint Francis de Sales and alongside the missionaries of Saint Francis de Sales of Annecy.

Oblates of Saint Francis de Sales

Also worthy of very special mention are the Oblates of Saint Francis de Sales (OSFS), founded at Troyes in France by

Father Louis Brisson (1817-1908). He was encouraged by the Visitation nun, the venerable Mary de Sales Chappuis, to initiate several apostolic works under the patronage of Saint Francis de Sales. In addition to the Oblate Fathers and Brothers, he founded the Oblate Sisters with Mother Francis de Sales Aviat. Associated with the Oblates of Saint Francis de Sales is a Secular de Sales Institute founded in 1944. The Oblates have spread to many parts of the world and are well established in the United States.

Katherine Burton, in her biography of Father Brisson, relates how he met Don Bosco:

Near the end of October 1881, with Father Deshairs, head of the Oblate school at Macon, he left for Italy, stopping first at Turin, for he had a great desire to see Don Bosco, founder of the Salesian Fathers, who had done much work among young people along lines similar to Father Brisson's, and of whose reputation for sanctity he had heard much.

Don Bosco received them with great simplicity and exquisite kindness. He took Father Brisson to his own room, high up in the old building. There were many steps to climb, and when Father Brisson was halfway up he was tired out, but he said nothing, for Don Bosco was going ahead with the springy step of a boy. They finally reached the top, and chairs, to Father Brisson's relief. "Why are you going to Rome?" Don Bosco asked. "Why don't you stay with us?"

"I am going to Rome to establish my religious just as you established yours."

"Oh, in that case I shall not keep you. But I am sorry. I think we would work well together."

The two men talked for a long time, telling each other of their difficulties of the past and present. Each had met difficulties that at times had all but compromised their work, and since the difficulties of both had been much the same, neither wanted to stop talking when the time came for Father Brisson to go.

"Well," said Don Bosco philosophically, "the cross which marks both our foundations with its divine seal—is it not the pledge of the blessing of the Lord?"

From Turin the travelers went directly to Rome, where Father Brisson was promptly granted an audience. When he first saw Leo XIII he noted the wonderful brilliance of his eyes, through which his mind seemed actually shining, he thought. When the pope surveyed his visitor for a moment and then smiled, Father Brisson had exactly the feeling he had had when

he was with Don Bosco, that a sense of sympathy flowed between them. He felt as much at home here as he had when he
had talked with Pius IX. (Burton, Katherine. *So Much, So
Soon*, 151-152)

Several passages in Burton's book deal with Father Brisson's work of education, based on Saint Francis de Sales and
similar to Don Bosco's own Preventive System. Describing
Father Brisson's method, she writes:

First, he urged on his teachers in both congregations a great
care in their handling of the children entrusted to them: they
must never smother a reasonable inclination to freedom, even
in the youngest. They must not destroy the child's sense of re-
sponsibility either. He counseled his teachers:

*Don't insist on your own opinions. Don't block natural inclinations, but
hold the child in high esteem and instead of frustrating, lend a hand to
the work which grace accomplishes in these young souls. The capital
point of Saint Francis de Sales's educational doctrine was respect for the
soul of the child, respect for the soul of youth. You may wonder how you
can respect an urchin who is not at all respectable—well, there is an old
saying:* Maxima puero debetur reverentia—*the highest respect is due to
a child.*

*The child understands you very well. He knows if you are treating
him with disdain or if you despise him—and later on he will not respect
his own soul if you have not respected it. He will not know his own
moral worth if you do not recognize it. There is good in every child.
There is some trace of baptismal grace. You will find that if you treat
him with respect and at the same time exercise your authority over him,
your power over him will be for good.*

He wanted his teachers to be so well grounded that they could
teach with certainty and ease. But he said he was equally anx-
ious to have them pray for these children, to keep them in their
daily prayers during the recitation of the breviary, at Mass,
during meditation: "Prayer for them will bring soundness to
your judgment, light to your intelligence, generosity and de-
votedness to your hearts."

As for the matter of discipline, he felt it was a thousand times
better to prevent childish infractions from happening than to
have to correct them. If the child misbehaved, the teacher must
never be angry with him, never humiliate him: "You should
leave him with the impression that care for his own good and
the interests of justice are the activating forces behind any
punishment. And of course to influence your pupils you must
yourselves give a good example. Your personal goodness and
personal recollection and personal mortification will affect the

child more deeply than many words with long sermons." (ibid., 137-138)

It is hardly surprising that Father Brisson and Don Bosco, both devotees of Saint Francis de Sales, should have adopted similar methods in the education of the young. It might be well at this point to compare the motto, "Live Jesus!" often used by Father Brisson and taken from Saint Francis de Sales, with that chosen by Don Bosco—*Da mihi animas!* Actually the two mottos are two sides of the same Salesian coin. Don Bosco's emphasis on zeal for souls is understood to spring from love; i.e., a deep spiritual union with Christ, in the spirit of Saint Paul: ". . . the life I live now is not my own; Christ is living in me." (Gal 2:20) The Oblate motto of life in Christ finds its most lively expression in intense labor for souls. Don Bosco's motto brings out the exterior manifestation; the Oblate motto expresses the interior motivation, which has priority. Saint Francis de Sales says this very well:

> We must begin with the interior. ". . . return to me," says God, "with your whole heart . . ." [Jl 2:12] The divine Spouse, in His invitation to the soul, says: "Set me as a seal on your heart, as a seal on your arm." [Sg 8:6] Yes, truly, for whosoever has Jesus Christ in his heart has him soon afterwards in all his exterior actions . . . (*Introduction* III, 23)

Whoever is united to the heart of Jesus, then, has a heart full of love which finds expression especially in acts of zeal for the salvation of the world, but which also gives rise to vital prayer by which every action is turned into an act of love of God. This emphasis on prayer is well expressed in the motto, "Live Jesus!" which de Sales designated as the motto for his own Visitation Order.

Visitation Sisters and Other Related Groups

The primary source of the influence of Francis de Sales in the Church since the saint's death has been the quiet but very effective presence of his spiritual daughters, the Sisters of the Visitation or Visitandines. As of this writing there are thirty-four Visitation monasteries in France, thirty-one in Italy and twenty-two in Spain. There are twenty-four other foundations in Europe, four in Africa and one in Lebanon. South America counts eighteen, Mexico and Central America seven, Canada three and the United States fifteen. (Like other religious, however, the Visitandines have suffered a decline in membership over the past few years.)

In Belgium in this century, another Visitation order arose called the Salesian Congregation of the Visitation, which joined together several groups desirous of living according to the spirit of Saint Francis de Sales.

Mention should also be made of the Daughters of Saint Francis de Sales, founded by the venerable Caroline Colchen-Carré de Malberg (1829-1891) in association with L'Abbé Henri Chaumont (1836-1896). The Daughters are divided into three distinct groups: the lay group, the sisters with vows, called the Salesian Missionaries of Mary Immaculate, and a third branch functioning as home missionaries, who take no vows but who live in community.

L'Abbé Chaumont also founded the Priests of Saint Francis de Sales (PSFS). The periodical *Jyothidhara*,[20] published in India, gives further information, summarized below.

A Large Family of 6000

One hundred years since its foundation, the spiritual family of Father Henri Chaumont and Mrs. Caroline Carré has spread to twenty countries of the world. Lay members (women, men, couples) form about half of the membership (3300). The ideal of Father Chaumont for the diverse groups, whether lay members, missionaries or diocesan priests, was "personal sanctification and the apostolate," which he considered inseparable.[21] The model for each member is Christ, who applied to himself the prophecy of Isaiah:

The spirit of the Lord is upon me;
therefore he has anointed me.
He has sent me to bring glad tidings to the poor . . . (Lk 4:18)

Each baptized person is called to holiness, and Chaumont's followers answer the call according to their lay, religious or priestly state. Father Chaumont was profoundly impressed by the role that the Holy Spirit played in the life of the apostles, as recorded in Acts, and by the help given to the apostles by the first Christians, according to their state in life. He determined to conform his societies to this apostolic tradition and chose

Francis de Sales as the saint most capable of inspiring and assisting modern Christians to live according to this ideal.

He looked upon Saint Francis de Sales as a human copy, as perfect as can be, of the Lord Jesus, "gentle and humble of heart." (Mt 11:29) "To live in the school of Saint Francis de Sales as an imitator of Jesus," he stated, "one must be led by the Spirit of Jesus." In this school we are taught "to be what we are, and to be it well, to give honor to our Maker," in the very vocation and place in which we are, with the real people who live with us, without dreaming of other people or places.

By a deep, interior union with Jesus in all that one does, through short prayers repeated interiorly while coming and going, every action becomes an act of love, in accordance with the principle of Saint Francis de Sales: "We must do all peacefully and out of love, nothing by force!" (*Jyothidhara*, Vol. VI, No. 3, July 1986)

It is easy to see in the above summary the affinity of spirit between Don Bosco, Father Brisson and L'Abbé Chaumont, all in perfect harmony with their common patron, Saint Francis de Sales. Father Chaumont's apostolic groups bear a striking resemblance to the vast project envisioned by Don Bosco in 1850. (See pages 37-38.)

Saint Francis de Sales and Other Religious Founders

The original intention of Francis de Sales to establish a religious congregation active in the world, which he changed because the idea was ahead of the times, gave inspiration to many religious societies, including secular institutes, which arose after his time up until our own day.

Vincent de Paul, who knew Francis de Sales, was able later in the same century to found the active religious congregations of the Vincentians and the Sisters of Charity. In his apostolic letter on Saint Francis de Sales, Pope Paul VI noted that the saint "also helped Pierre de Berulle, Saint John Eudes and John Olier, all three of whom were educators of the French clergy and for whom he was a precursor." He inspired them by "his magnificent authority and the warmth of his spirit, which was said to be almost divine."

The founder of the Brothers of the Christian Schools, Saint John Baptist de la Salle (1651-1719), placed his work of education under the patronage of Saint Francis de Sales and visited the saint's tomb. He chose his motto "Live Jesus!" and wanted it repeated after each exercise during the day's schedule. Impressed by the Christian humanism of de Sales, Saint John saw the vocation of teaching as the *opus Dei* for his followers.

The Brigidine Sisters and the Patrician Brothers, founded by Bishop Daniel Delaney (1747-1814) consider the *via media* of work-prayer as their ideal, following the Salesian "ecstasy of action." The Presentation Sisters, founded by Nano Nagle (1718-1784), look upon holiness as the simple fulfillment of small, daily duties done with intense love; Saint Francis de Sales was a principal influence in the spiritual growth of the foundress and her congregation. The Good Samaritan Sisters, founded by the Benedictine Bishop John Polding (1794-1877) in Australia, followed the same pattern: their rule expressly states that the writings and teachings of Saint Francis de Sales would constitute the substance of their daily spiritual reading. The Irish Christian Brothers, founded by Edmund Ignatius Rice (1762-1844), were deeply influenced by the Jesuit spirituality of Saint Ignatius, yet "the spirit of faith and purity of intention" that was stressed for their work was taken from Saint Francis de Sales. The Sisters of Saint Joseph of Carondelet, founded by Jean-Paul Medaille (1618-1689), and the Mercy Sisters, founded by Catherine McAuley in 1827, also hold Saint Francis de Sales in honor and take inspiration from him. Saint Theresa of the Child Jesus, whose "little way" is well known, was influenced in her spirituality by her elder sister, Mother Agnes, who had been a pupil of the Visitation Sisters. Francis himself had been greatly influenced in his own lifetime by the Carmelite spirituality of Saint Teresa of Avila.

The English-Speaking World

The influence of Saint Francis de Sales has been felt in countless ways in the English-speaking world. Even during the saint's lifetime the *Introduction* was translated into English and praised by King James I, although he was not a Catholic. In succeeding centuries the saint's influence continued through Bishop Challoner (1691-1781), who left a vast and varied literary legacy to English Catholics. Before this time, Richard Smith, bishop of Chalcedon and ordinary of England, recommended to his secular priests in 1630 the use of mental prayer and instructed them to train the laity in the Salesian method, using the *Introduction* as their textbook. Other instances of the influence of the saint have been brought forward by Eamon Duffy.[22] Nor should we forget in more modern times the poet Francis Thompson, so devoted to Francis de Sales, who found in the saint's writings the inspiration for *The Hound of Heaven*.

The Dispersion of the Salesian Spirit

As the spirit of Saint Francis de Sales has captivated numerous religious founders and inspired many saintly persons to establish distinct Salesian families, so the Salesian spirit of Don Bosco has given rise within the Church to additional religious congregations founded by alumni, priests or bishops who belonged to Don Bosco's Society of Saint Francis de Sales. Presently we can count no fewer than seventeen, and the number keeps increasing. (See center pages of book and Appendix 2 for additional information.)

This chapter on the nineteenth century would be incomplete without mention of two ecclesiastics greatly devoted to Saint Francis de Sales. The first was Gaspard Mermillot (1824-1892), Swiss cardinal and a pioneer in modern Catholic social movements. He built the Church of Notre Dame at Geneva between 1851 and 1859 with funds subscribed from all parts of Christendom. As a bishop he was especially active in the cause of Catholic education and cooperated with Father Brisson in founding the Oblate Sisters of Saint Francis de Sales at Troyes for the protection of poor working girls. In 1873, when the pope appointed him vicar apostolic of Geneva, he was exiled from Switzerland, where he had previously worked quite successfully. (He met Don Bosco in 1876—see page 56.) He was famous as both a preacher and a writer. Pope Leo XIII named him a cardinal in 1890.

Another nineteenth-century prelate greatly esteemed by Pope Pius IX was the Frenchman Louis Gaston de Ségur (1820-1881). Among his manifold undertakings for the Church was the Saint Francis de Sales Association for the Defense and Preservation of the Faith. After founding this pious society in 1859, he established it in forty dioceses of France in less than a year. Ségur became widely known for his spiritual and apologetic works, which fill ten volumes. His theological outlook was that of Bérulle and others of the seventeenth-century French school of spirituality, combined with that of Saint Francis de Sales, always his favorite saint.

15
The Esteem of Twentieth-Century Popes for Saint Francis de Sales

Pius XI and Paul VI

In the twentieth century two papal documents have been written on Saint Francis de Sales, one by Pius XI (*Rerum Omnium* in 1923) and the other by Paul VI (*Subaudiae Gemma* in 1967), commemorating respectively the centenaries of the death (1622) and birth (1567) of the saint.

Good Pope John

Pope John XXIII, who attracted the whole world by his gentleness, had Saint Francis de Sales as his model. When still a seminarian, he wrote in his journal:

> Today was a perfect feast; I spent it in the company of Saint Francis de Sales, gentlest of saints! What a magnificent figure of a man, priest and bishop! If I were like him, I would not mind even if they were to make me pope! I love to let my thoughts dwell on him, on his goodness and on his teaching. I have read his life so many times! His counsels are so acceptable to my

heart. By the light of his example I feel more inclined toward humility, gentleness and calm. My life, so the Lord tells me, must be a perfect copy of that of Saint Francis de Sales, if I wish to bear good fruit. There is nothing extraordinary in me or in my behavior, except my way of doing ordinary things—"all ordinary things but done in no ordinary way." A great, a burning love for Jesus Christ and His Church; unalterable serenity of mind; wonderful gentleness with my fellow human beings— that is all!

O my loving saint, as I kneel before you at this moment, there is so much I could say to you! I love you tenderly and I will always remember you and look to you for help. O Saint Francis, I can say no more; you can see into my heart; give me what I need to become like you. (Roncalli, Giuseppe. *Journal of a Soul*, 110)

The future pope, as time was to prove, did imitate the gentleness of Saint Francis de Sales, earning the title, "Good Pope John." He retained a devotion to the bishop of Geneva throughout his life.

The Smiling Pope

The "Smiling Pope," John Paul I, when still a cardinal, addressed himself to Francis de Sales in his book, *Illustrissimi*:

I have reread a book which concerns you: *Saint Francis de Sales, Theologian of Love*. It was written some time ago by Henry Bordeaux of the Academy of France.

Before that, however, you yourself wrote that you had a "heart of flesh," which was moved, which understood, which kept reality in mind and knew that men are not pure spirits but feeling creatures. With this human heart you loved reading and the arts, you wrote with the most refined sensitivity, even encouraging your friend Bishop Camus to write novels. You leaned toward all, to give all something.

Already as a university student in Padua, you made a rule for yourself never to avoid or curtail a conversation with anyone, no matter how unlikable and boring; to be modest and without insolence, free and without austerity, gentle without affectation, pliant and without dissent.

You kept your word. To your father, who had chosen a rich and pretty heiress as your wife, you amiably replied: "Papa, I have seen mademoiselle, but she deserves better than me!"

Priest, missionary, bishop, you gave your time to others: the young, the poor, the sick, sinners, heretics, bourgeois, noble ladies, prelates, princes.

Like everyone, you were sometimes misunderstood, contradicted. The "heart of flesh" suffered, but went on loving the contradictors. "If an enemy were to put out my right eye," you once said, "I would want to smile at him with my left; if he put out both my eyes, I would still have a heart to love him."

Many would consider this a peak. For you, the peak is something else. You wrote, in fact: "Man is the perfection of the universe; the spirit is the perfection of man; love is the perfection of the spirit; the love of God is the perfection of love." Therefore the peak, the perfection, the excellence of the universe is, for you, loving God. (Luciani, Albino Cardinal. *Illustrissimi*, 103-104)

John Paul II

In his visit to France in the fall of 1986, Pope John Paul spoke at length of Saint Francis de Sales both at Lyons and at Annecy. At Lyons the pope proclaimed Francis de Sales as a model for bishops because he was so "completely available to all his people." During the Mass at Annecy, he used the chalice of the saint and extolled him as a "precursor of Vatican Council II."

Pope John Paul highlights the principal virtues of Saint Francis de Sales in these passages taken from the English edition of the *Osservatore Romano*.

Expert in Humanity

One could well apply to him the title of "expert in humanity" which Paul VI claimed for the Church. For in the intellectual ferment of his time, which he observed with sympathy, Francis de Sales knew how to proceed with clear discernment; he was penetrated above all by respect for man and for his liberty. As a consequence, he interested himself in securing a balanced education for boys and girls.

Whatever the debate or negotiation in which he was involved, people found in him a reconciler, free from all partisan spirit, a man of peace.

When his people suffered violence, he knew how to raise his voice in their defense, without taking account of the criticism he would incur, because he set his words and his actions unambiguously in the evangelical realm of charity. May we today, who are confronted by unrest and violence and by too many attacks on human life and dignity, deserve for our episcopal ministry the title that the simple faithful gave to Francis de Sales: "the author of peace."

Doctor of Love

Saint Francis de Sales was the Doctor of Love who unceasingly emphasized the living spring from which flows the covenant of God with men: God loves us; God accompanies us, at each stage of life, with a patient and faithful love; God inspires in us His own desire for what is good, an attraction to what is beautiful and true. In His providence, God gives us life, so that we may exist in His image and likeness. God calls us to share always what constitutes the greatness of His own life—perfect love. He gives us interior freedom and makes us capable of tasting the certainty that we are loved and of resolving firmly to respond to this love.

Brothers and sisters, this great bishop knew also man's weakness and his difficulty in responding with constant faith to the message of love of the covenant. He knew that we often look for the power to love more in ourselves than in a generous welcome of the gift that comes from God. This is why Francis de Sales never wearied in demonstrating to his brothers the patience and the tenderness of God, who is ready to forgive and to save.

Servant of the Church

Returning unceasingly to the love of God that we live thanks to Christ, Francis de Sales takes his place within the great tradition expressed thus by Saint Augustine: "For us, to live is to love—*vita nostra dilectio est.*" (Enarr. in Ps. 54, n. 7) He himself writes: "Everything is of love, in love, for love and from love in the Holy Church." (O IV, 4) As a great servant of the Church, he acted always in this spirit.

. . . [In his time] with a problem different from today's situation, endless debates took place about the role and authority of the bishop of Rome. I shall single out the final point that was the conclusion of Francis de Sales's analysis of the question: one must preach calmly—he says, "sweetly"—these two points: ecclesiastical and Christian unity, love and devotion to the Holy See, which is the bond of this union and ecclesiastical communion. (Letter to Mons. Germonio, March 1612.)

Generous Pastor

Francis de Sales loved the people he served as pastor. He gave himself entirely to the task of leading them on the paths of the

Gospel. In his pastoral activity, Francis de Sales had an acute sense of the mission that is incumbent on each bishop. He knew that the service of unity is a priority in this mission. He had to carry out this service in a time when a grave rupture had broken out among the Christians of his region. In the climate that was dominant then, he carried out this service with all his faith, all his love, all his generosity. May the Lord inspire the dialogue in which we find ourselves today, as brothers who are still separated! May he strengthen in us a common will for reconciliation in truth and love, so that we may soon find again the unity that we so much desire!

Conciliator

Francis de Sales, who was endowed with a great discernment in meetings wih individuals, entered also into the affairs and the debates of his time, with a moderation that aroused confidence. He deserved to be called the "conciliator." In his involvement in the theological discussions or in the conflicts of the city, he heeded the appeal of the Psalm: ". . . seek peace, and follow after it" (Ps 34:15), or that maxim of Proverbs:

A patient man is better than a warrior,
and he who rules his temper, than he who takes a city.
(Prv 16:32)

Patron of Journalists

Among the saints who have brought the message of the Gospel to their contemporaries in so many ways, Francis de Sales belongs to the group of those who have discovered a langauge that is wonderfully appropriate. We would say today that he was a man of communication. In his letters and in his books, he held one's attenion with a style that revealed both his spiritual experience and his deep knowledge of men. As the patron of journalists, of those who have the mission of writing, may he inspire their work in a clear knowledge of those whom they are addressing, in the fraternal respect of those with whom they are sharing the truth!

Devoted to Mary

In his reflection on the love of God, Francis de Sales recognized in Mary the unique perfection in this love. He had dedicated his work to her. He said one day: "How good it is to be the child, although unworthy, of this glorious mother . . ." I entrust all . . . to her whom Saint Francis de Sales called "this sweet mother of hearts, this mother of holy love." (L 936; *Osservatore Romano*, November 10, 1986, 13-15)

16
Epilogue

One hundred years after the death of Saint John Bosco, the name Salesian is known throughout the world. Don Bosco and Salesian are synonymous.

So what's in a name? Is this the critical question that scholars are asking about the depths of the relationship between Don Bosco and Saint Francis de Sales? If so, the answer is simple. The name Salesian indicates the very spirit of Don Bosco, which is the spirit of Francis de Sales. It is a manifestation in our time of the Holy Spirit, lovingly and ardently at work in the world.

Certainly Saint Francis de Sales has not lost his own identity and importance in the Church. More than ever, he stands forth as the Doctor of the Church who is especially suited for modern times. He is the gentleman saint, a shining example of kindness and patience for people of all walks of life. The testimony of the popes and the myriad groups of his followers amply demonstrate this.

On the other hand, Saint John Bosco has achieved a similar preeminence in the Church. He worked tirelessly for the material and spiritual good of the underclasses of society—the young, the poor, the orphaned, the illiterate. He taught a Salesian spirituality that was suitable to schoolchildren, workers, storekeepers and government officials. He was a contemplative in action, with eyes fixed on heaven and feet planted firmly on earth.

It is clear from the evidence presented in this book that Don Bosco loved Saint Francis de Sales, that he was inspired by his spirituality, and that he shared the same spirit with his Salesians and adopted it in his apostolate for youth.

One can follow Saint Francis de Sales without following Don Bosco, but one cannot follow Don Bosco without following Saint Francis de Sales. This, I think, is one of the most important messages that Don Bosco gives as a memento to all his Salesians on the occasion of the centenary of his death.

How much did Saint Francis de Sales influence Don Bosco? In recent years there has been considerable scholarly research in the Salesian Congregation to seek an answer to this question. Studies along these lines will no doubt continue.

It is difficult to measure spiritual realities with the tangible criteria that are often demanded by critical minds. Although the present book does not lack its own scholarly apparatus, it is more a *witness* than a proof of its main thesis; namely, that understanding the spirit of Saint Francis de Sales is an essential rather than an accidental component in understanding Don Bosco's own spirit. This life-witness, together with the illustrious example of numerous members of Don Bosco's society—modeled on the founder's own devotion to Saint Francis de Sales—is a very powerful premise in itself. *Contra factum non datur argumentum*: it is hard to disprove a fact, especially in the realm of spiritual realities.

The worldwide, spiritual influence of the Salesians of Don Bosco is indisputable evidence of the binding link between Saint Francis de Sales and Saint John Bosco.

Francis J. Klauder, SDB

Appendix 1

Devotions in Honor of Saint Francis de Sales and Saint John Bosco

Recommendation to God (Practiced by Saint Francis de Sales)

I recommend myself to You, O my God. I place myself entirely, with all that belongs to me, into the hands of Your eternal Goodness. I beg You to look upon me as being completely given up to You. I leave You absolutely the care of my person, what I am and what You wish me to be. To You do I recommend my soul, my mind, my heart, my memory, my understanding, my will. Grant me the grace that with all these faculties of my being I may serve You, love You, please You and adore You forever. (These and other practices may be found in *In the Midst of the World* by Sr. Joanna Marie Wenzel)

The Litany of Saint Francis de Sales[23]

Lord, have mercy on us.
Christ, have mercy on us.
Lord, have mercy on us.
Christ, hear us.
Christ, graciously hear us.
God the Father of Heaven, have mercy on us.
God the Son, Redeemer of the world, have mercy on us.
God the Holy Spirit, have mercy on us.
Holy Trinity, one God, have mercy on us.
Saint Francis de Sales, admirable bishop,
   [Response: Pray for us.]
Saint Francis de Sales, beloved by God,
Saint Francis de Sales, imitator of Jesus Christ,
Saint Francis de Sales, filled with the gifts of the Lord,
Saint Francis de Sales, favorite of the mother of God,
Saint Francis de Sales, most devout to the saints,
Saint Francis de Sales, burning with love for the cross
   of Christ,

Saint Francis de Sales, most closely united to the divine will,
Saint Francis de Sales, vessel of election,
Saint Francis de Sales, light of the Church,
Saint Francis de Sales, perfect model of religious,
Saint Francis de Sales, source of wisdom,
Saint Francis de Sales, defender of the Catholic faith,
Saint Francis de Sales, good shepherd of the people,
Saint Francis de Sales, incomparable preacher,
Saint Francis de Sales, scourge of heresy,
Saint Francis de Sales, salt of the earth,
Saint Francis de Sales, model of justice,
Saint Francis de Sales, mirror of humility,
Saint Francis de Sales, despiser of the worldly spirit,
Saint Francis de Sales, lover of poverty,
Saint Francis de Sales, conqueror of carnal passions,
Saint Francis de Sales, terror of devils,
Saint Francis de Sales, merciful support of penitents,
Saint Francis de Sales, refuge of sinners,
Saint Francis de Sales, help of the poor,
Saint Francis de Sales, consoler of the afflicted,
Saint Francis de Sales, example of perfection,
Saint Francis de Sales, ark of holiness,
Saint Francis de Sales, imitator of the purity of the angels,
Saint Francis de Sales, cherub of wisdom,
Saint Francis de Sales, seraph of love,
Saint Francis de Sales, our holy patriarch,
Saint Francis de Sales, our sweet light,
Saint Francis de Sales, our mighty protector,
Saint Francis de Sales, our guide in the ways of God,
Saint Francis de Sales, our refuge,
Saint Francis de Sales, emulator of the angels,
Saint Francis de Sales, imitator of the apostles,
Saint Francis de Sales, sharer in the glory of the martyrs,
Saint Francis de Sales, glory of holy confesssors,
Saint Francis de Sales, teacher and director of virgins,
Saint Francis de Sales, glorious fellow-citizen of all the saints,
Lamb of God, You take away the sins of the world, spare us, O Lord.

Lamb of God, You take away the sins of the world, graciously hear us, O Lord.

Lamb of God, You take away the sins of the world, have mercy on us.

V. Pray for us, Saint Francis de Sales.

R. Make us worthy of the promises of Christ.

Let us pray.

Father, you gave Francis de Sales the spirit of compassion to befriend all men and women on the way to salvation. By his example, lead us to show your gentle love in the service of our fellow human beings. We ask this through Christ our Lord. Amen.

General Intercessions

Lord, you have given Don Bosco as father and teacher of youth.

May we, like him, be signs and bearers of your love for youth.

Response: Lord, hear our prayer.

Lord, render fruitful with your grace our apostolic work.

May we imitate the zeal and gentle charity of Saint Francis de Sales.

Lord, stir up in many youths a generous response to your call.

So that the Salesian Society through pastoral charity may continue its mission of salvation.

Lord, bless the several Salesian families within your Church.

May they be a powerful witness to the universal call to holiness in the midst of the world.

Lord, through the intercession of Mary, Mother of the Church and Help of Christians, inflame the hearts of all Christians with zeal for the salvation of the world.

Send forth Your Spirit and renew the face of the earth!

Appendix 2

Religious Congregations Which Have Originated from the Salesian Society of Saint John Bosco

Women

1. Volunteers of Don Bosco, founded by Father Rinaldi in Italy in 1917
2. Sisters of the Annunciation of Our Lord, founded by Blessed Versiglia and his successor, Bishop Canazei, in China in 1931
3. Daughters of Charity, founded by Father Cavoli in Japan in 1939
4. Missionaries of Mary Help of Christians, founded by Bishop Ferrando in India in 1942
5. Daughters of the Immaculate Conception, founded by Bishop Tavella in Argentina in 1947
6. Josephite Sisters, founded by Bishop De Almeida in Brazil in 1948
7. Sisters of Mary Immaculate, founded by Bishop LaRavoire Morrow in India in 1949
8. Daughters of the Queenship of Mary Immaculate, founded by Father Della Torre in Thailand in 1954
9. Salesian Oblates of the Sacred Heart, founded by Bishop Cognata in Italy in 1959
10. Missionaries of the Good Jesus, founded by Bishop Chavez in Brazil in 1963
11. Handmaids of the Immaculate Heart of Mary, founded by Bishop Pasotti in Thailand in 1964
12. Daughters of the Sacred Hearts of Jesus and Mary, founded by Father Variara, Apostle of Lepers, in Colombia in 1964
13. Daughters of the Divine Savior, founded by Bishop Aparicio in El Salvador in 1972
14. Messengers of Holy Mary, founded by Bishop Campelo in Brazil in 1973

Men

1. Sons of Divine Providence, founded by Blessed Orione in 1893
2. Servants of Charity, founded by Blessed Guanella in 1908
3. Society of Christ, founded by Cardinal Hlond in 1932

Addresses for Further Information about the Various Salesian Families

Visitation Sisters
2002 Bancroft Parkway
Wilmington, DE 19806

Visitation Sisters
Salesian Living Heritage
2455 Visitation Drive
Mendota Heights, MN 55120

Daughters of Mary Help
of Christians
(Salesian Sisters)
655 Belmont Avenue
Haledon, NJ 07508

Salesian Cooperators and
Salesians of Don Bosco
148 Main Street
New Rochelle, NY 10802

Volunteers of Don Bosco
202 Union Avenue
Paterson, NJ 07502

De Sales Secular Institute
Rev. John Connery, OSFS
1120 Blue Ball Road
Childs, MD 21916

Oblates of Saint Francis
de Sales
Public Relations Office
220 Kentmere Parkway
Wilmington, DE 19899

Fransalians (MSFS)
Salesianum
Visakhapatnam 530 003
Andhra Pradesk, India

**Lay Groups of
Saint Francis de Sales**

De Sales Resource Center
4421 Lower River Rd.
Stella Niagara, NY 14144

Salesian Advisor
1621 Otis St. N.E.
Washington, DC 20018

The Fraternity of Saint
Francis de Sales
2339 Nebraska Ave. N.W.
Washington, DC 20016

The Society of Saint Francis
de Sales
948 Masonridge Rd.
St. Louis, MO 63141

Notes

1   Pedrini's book in Italian is divided into two parts with two appendices, one for each part. The first appendix is itself divided into parts I and II. The English text's division into fifteen chapters considerably alters Pedrini's arrangement. Part I of his first appendix has become chapter 1 in the present work. Chapters 2, 3, 4, 5, 6, 10, 11 and 12 draw their materials from his introduction and the first part of his book. Chapter 8, dealing with the Salesian spirit, is treated in Pedrini's work from pages 76 to 81 and again from pages 121 to 125, all from the first part, including part II of the first appendix. The second part of Pedrini's book is covered by our chapters 7 and 13. His second appendix as written is omitted, although some of its content is incorporated into the English text. Chapters 9, 14 and 15 have been added, with materials drawn from various sources as indicated in each case. Pedrini has made use of the main sources of the writings of Saint John Bosco. There are two distinct collections: (1) the Caviglia collection, with commentary (1929, 1964); (2) the LAS collection (1976-1977). In addition, a collection of Don Bosco's unedited works is in progress at the Centro Studi Don Bosco at the Salesian Pontifical University (UPS) in Rome.

2   Bosco, Don. *Storia ecclesiastica ad uso della gioventù*, 356-358; cf. Caviglia, Alberto. *Don Bosco opere*, vol. 1, parte II, 451-454.

3   cf. *Oeuvres de Saint François de Sales*. Chief English translations of the saint's principal works are: (1) *Introduction to the Devout Life*, newly translated with an introduction and notes by John K. Ryan. (2) *Treatise on the Love of God*, translated with an introduction and notes by John K. Ryan, in 2 volumes. More recent publications on Saint Francis de Sales include: (1) *In the Midst of the World*, by Sister Joanna Marie Wenzel, VHM. (2) *The Spiritual Directory of Saint Francis de Sales*, edited by Rev. Lewis Fiorelli, OSFS. (3) *Sermons of Saint Francis de Sales*, edited by Rev. Lewis Fiorelli, OSFS. (4) *Every Day with Saint Francis de Sales*, edited by Francis J. Klauder, SDB. (5) *Bond of Perfection*, by Wendy Wright.

4   cf. Bosco, Don. *Opere edite*, vol. 3, 215-500.

5   The original words of Saint Francis de Sales are recorded in *Année Sainte*, 10, 257, as follows: ". . . et puis, ma che're fille, voudrez-vous bien qu'en un courraux d'un quart d'heure je misse, à bas ce pauvre petit edifice de paix interieure, auquel je travaille par un prit fait particulier depuis dix-huit ans?"

6   See *By Love Compelled: The Life of Father Philip Rinaldi*, by Peter Rinaldi, SDB, 117-118.

7   For more detailed references see the Italian edition of Father Pedrini's book, *San Francesco di Sales e Don Bosco*, 34-35.

8   These *Acts*, issued at the time from the Salesian motherhouse in Turin, now originate from the Salesian generalate in Rome.

9   The counsels recommended by Don Bosco are reported in Father Viganò's letter commemorating the centenary of Saint Mary Mazzarello, February 24, 1981.

10   The sayings of Saint Francis de Sales are taken from an unpublished manuscript composed by Father Wallace Cornell, SDB. Father Cornell's *Reflections from a Seasoned Soul*, which consists of quotations from Saint Francis de Sales, is available from Salesiana Publishers, P.O. Box 838 MCPO, Makati, Metro Manila 3117, Philippines.

11   This important theme is taken up again in chapter 9.

12   See the *Salesian Special General Chapter 20*, Rome, 1972, 80-81, 85-86.

13   For Valentini's writings on the subject in question see *Salesianum*, vol. 14, 1952, 129-152 and *Rivista di pedagogia e scienze religiose*, vol. 1, 1967, 3-47.

14   Quoted in *Biblioteca di scienze religiose*, No. 17, "Spiritualità dell'azione," 183.

15   Ceria, Eugenio. *Il cooperatori Salesiani*, 59.

16   See also de Burgh, D. J., *Francis and John*, p. 23, for a narrative of the incident in English. Note also that the church was St. Stephen of the Greeks, which is no longer standing, but the statue of the Black Madonna has been preserved in the church of the monks of St. Thomas of Villanova.

17   Orione later became a priest, founded a religious order and was beatified by Pope John Paul II in 1980, forty years after his death.

18   See note 8.

19   Our correlation is not meant to be restrictive. Father Viganò, for instance, returns to relevant themes of Salesian spirituality according to current needs. The 1987 *Catholic Almanac*, p. 64, in its News Events for 1985, carries the following comment on the topic, "Criticism of the Pope," as treated in a letter of Father Viganò to the Salesians:
     Those who "dissent from or pay no attention to pastoral guidelines of the pope contribute to the weakening among people of his charism of ecclesial direction," said the major superior of the Salesians in a letter to the 17,000 members of the order. "At the present day, we are witnessing disastrous consequences of criticism of the pope" and dissent from his teachings, especially concerning moral values. Be-

cause of such criticism, "one sees public opinion getting even further away from the very foundations of Christian morality, to such an extent that the ethical criterion is no longer the Gospel but statistics, the civil law, or manners of behavior accepted by society . . . The harm caused to people, and especially to young people, by pastoral workers and professors who oppose, undervalue or mock the pastoral direction of the present successor of Peter, is serious from a pastoral point of view." He called on Salesians not to have an "anti-Roman complex" and not to be parties to "a growing animosity to this pope of the present day."

20   In addition to the reference in the text, see the French periodical, *La tradition vivante* (Noel, 1981), "François de Sales, Prophete de l'Amour," Editions C.I.F., 209 Route de Saint'Leu 93800 Epinay-sur-Seine, France. Other congregations or associations animated by the spirit of Saint Francis de Sales are the Sisters of Charity of St. Joan Antida Thouret (1765-1826) and various confraternities "more numerous than others in the Church," according to the famous Dominican scholar and expert on Saint Francis de Sales, E.J. Lajeunie (died 1964) in *Saint François de Sales*. Father Pedrini (11 ff) mentions also the Sisters of Saint Francis de Sales of Padua, the Salesian Sisters of the Sacred Heart of Lecce and the Salesian Oblate Sisters of the Sacred Heart of Tivoli.

21   In 1984 Father Viganò commemorated the fiftieth anniversary of Don Bosco's canonization and noted that his holiness, too, was inseparable from the apostolate. He quoted Don Paul Albera's letter of October 18, 1920 (L 366):
Don Albera describes our founder's holiness well when he says that for him "religious perfection and the apostolate were one and the same thing," and Don Bosco clearly showed that God was his all-in-all by being always totally available for the mission of Christ and his Church.
In my circular letter on the Salesian family (ASC, No. 304, 1982) I endeavored to analyze that kind of supernatural love, that pastoral charity, that was peculiar to Don Bosco: his powerful spirit of union, the unique ethos of our religious consecration, and the living spring of our holiness.
It is essential that our hearts beat in time with his to the rhythm of Da mihi animas. *I hope we can reach out to the reality beyond this metaphor and understand the practical significance and crucial scintilla that gives meaning to our whole way of holiness: a life of pastoral charity that finds its outlet in a predilection for the young and is characterized by kindess.*

22   *Clergy Review*, Dec. 1981, 449-454.

23   We reproduce here a litany in English, published for private use in 1955 in the *Visitation Manual* by the Sisters of the Visitation and

again in 1959 by the Oblates of Saint Francis de Sales in Father Woods's *Spiritual Directory*. In Pedrini's book (162-166) there are two other litanies, one in French by the curate of Saint Sulpice (1858) and the other in Latin, published by the Salesians of Don Bosco in 1906, during the time of Blessed Michael Rua.

Bibliography

Amadei, Angelo. *Don Bosco e il suo apostolato*. Torino: SEI, 1949.

———, ed. *Memorie biografiche di S. Giovanni Bosco*. Vol. 10. Torino: S. Benigno Canavese, 1939.

Ambrosio, Pietro and Raffaele, Farina, eds. *Opere edite di San Giovanni Bosco*. 37 vols. Roma: LAS, 1976-1977.

Année Sainte des Religieuses de la Visitation Sainte Marie. 12 vols. Annecy, 1867-1871.

Aubry, Joseph, SDB. *The Renewal of Our Salesian Life*. Translated by Paul Bedard, SDB. 2 vols. New Rochelle, NY: Don Bosco Publications, 1984.

Auffray, A. *Saint John Bosco*. London: Burns, Oates and Washbourne, Ltd., 1930.

Bibliografia Salesiana: opere e scritti riguardanti San Francesco di Sales (1623-1955). Brasier, E., Morganti, M. and St. Dorica, M., eds. Torino: SEI, 1956.

Bonetti, G. *Saint John Bosco's Early Apostolate*. London: Burns, Oates and Washbourne, Ltd., 1934.

Borgatello, Diego, SDB, ed. and trans. *Biographical Memoirs of Saint John Bosco*. New Rochelle, NY: Salesiana Publishers, 1965-.

Bosco, Don. *Opere edite: ristampa anastatica; prima serie; libri e opuscoli*. 37 vols. Roma: LAS, 1976-1977.

———. *Storia ecclesiastica ad uso della gioventù*. Torino: S. Benigno Canavese, 1877.

Cafasso, Joseph. *Manuscripts*. Rome: Archives of the Salesian Congregation, n.d.

Camus, Jean Pierre. *The Spirit of Saint Francis de Sales*. Edited by C. F. Kelley. New York: Harper, 1952.

Caviglia, Alberto, ed. *Opere e scritte edite e inedite di Don Bosco*. 6 vols. Torino: SEI, 1929-1943; 2nd edition, 1964-1965.

Ceria, Eugenio. *Il cooperatori Salesiani*. Torino: SEI, 1952.

———, *The Salesian Society*. Edited by Joseph G. E. Hopkins. New Rochelle: Salesiana Publishers, 1955.

———, ed. *Annali della società Salesiana*. 3 vols. Torino: SEI, 1946.

———, ed. *Epistolario di San Giovanni Bosco*. 4 vols. Torino: SEI, 1955-1958.

———, ed. *Memorie biografiche del Beato Giovanni Bosco*. vols. 11-15. Torino: SEI, 1930-1934.

———, ed. *Memorie biografiche di San Giovanni Bosco*. vols. 16-19. Torino: SEI, 1935-1939.

———, ed. *Memorie dell'Oratorio di San Francesco di Sales dal 1815 al 1855*. Torino: SEI, 1946.

Cornell, W. L., SDB. *Don Bosco: Spiritual Director of Young People*. Metro Manila, Philippines: Salesiana Publishers, 1986.

_____. *Reflections from a Seasoned Soul*. Metro Manila, Philippines: Salesiana Publishers, n.d.

de Burgh, D. J. *Francis and John*. California: Benziger Sisters Publ., 1979.

de Sales, Francis. *The Catholic Controversy*. Translated by Henry Benedict Mackey, OSB, under the direction of John Cuthbert Hedley, OSB. *Library of Saint Francis de Sales*, vol. 3. London and New York: Burns and Oates, 1886.

_____. *Introduction to the Devout Life*. Translated by John K. Ryan. New York: Harper and Row, 1966.

_____. *The Mystical Explanation of the Canticle of Canticles*. Translated by Henry Benedict and Canon Mackey, OSB. London: Burns and Oates, Ltd., 1908.

_____. *Oeuvres de Saint François de Sales: Edition d'aprés les autographes et les éditions originales*. 26 vols. Annecy: Monastére de la Visitation, 1892-1932.

_____. *Treatise on the Love of God*. Translated by John K. Ryan. 2 vols. New York: Image Books, 1963; Rockford, IL: Tan Books, 1975.

_____. *On the Preacher and Preaching*. Translated by John K. Ryan. Chicago: Henry Regnery Co., 1964.

_____. *Saint Francis de Sales: Selected Letters*. Translated by Elisabeth Stopp. New York: Harper, 1960.

_____. *Sermons of Saint Francis de Sales*. Translated by the Nuns of the Visitation. Edited by Rev. Lewis Fiorelli, OSFS. Rockford, IL: Tan Books, 1985.

_____. *The Spiritual Conferences*. Translated under the supervision of Abbot Gasquet and Canon Mackey, OSB. London: Burns, Oates and Washbourne, Ltd., 1923.

Favini, Don. *Alle fonti della vita salesiana*. Torino: SEI, 1965.

Fiorelli, Lewis J., OSFS. *The Spiritual Directory of Saint Francis de Sales*. Boston: Daughters of St. Paul, 1986.

Giraudi, F. *L'Oratorio di Don Bosco*. Torino: SEI, 1935.

Hermans, Francis. *Histoire doctrinale de l'humanisme chrétien*. 4 vols. Paris: Casterman, 1948.

Klauder, Francis J., SDB, ed. *Every Day with Saint Francis de Sales*. New Rochelle, NY: Don Bosco Publications, 1985.

Lajeunie, Etienne-Marie. *Saint François de Sales et l'esprit Salesien*. Paris: Seuil, 1962.

_____. *Saint Francis de Sales*. Translated by Rory Sullivan, OSFS. Bangalore, India: S.F.S. Publications, 1986.

Lemoyne, G.B., ed. *Memorie biografiche di Don Giovanni Bosco; Memorie biografiche del venerabile servo di Dio Don Giovanni Bosco*. Vols. 1-9. Torino: S. Benigno Canavese, 1898-1917.

Luciani, Albino Cardinal. *Illustrissimi*. Boston: Little, Brown and Company, 1978.

Marceau, William. *Optimism in the Works of Saint Francis de Sales*. Visakhapatnam, India: S.F.S. Publications, 1983.

Maritan, Jacques. *True Humanism*. New York: Scribner's, 1938.

McPake, Martin, SDB. *A Simple Commentary on the Constitutions.* Madras, India: The Citadel, 1981.

Pedrini, Arnold, SDB. *San Francesco di Sales e Don Bosco.* Roma: UPS, 1983.

Picca, J. and Strús, J. *San Francesco de Sales e i Salesiani di Don Bosco.* Roma: LAS, 1986.

Ricaldone, Pietro. *Don Bosco Educatore.* 2 vols. Colle Don Bosco: LDC, 1951.

———, *La Pietà.* Colle Don Bosco: LDC, 1951.

Rinaldi, Peter, SDB. *By Love Compelled: The Life of Father Philip Rinaldi.* New Rochelle, NY: Salesiana Publishers, n.d.

Roncalli, Giuseppe. *Journal of a Soul.* New York: McGraw-Hill, 1965.

Sage, Pierre. "Humanisme chrétien." *Catholicisme* 5: col. 1072-1077.

Salesian Studies. Authors include:

> Congar, Yves, OP. "Francis de Sales Today." Vol 2, No. 1, pp. 5-9.
>
> Lux, Otto, OSFS. "Augustinian Influence in the Ethics of Francis de Sales." Vol. 3, No. 3, pp. 52-67; No. 4, pp. 89-99.
>
> Murphy, Ruth. "Saint Francis de Sales and Culture." Vol. 4, No. 4, pp. 30-47.
>
> Paul VI, Pope. "Subaudiae Gemma." Vol. 4, No. 2, pp. 69-80.
>
> Pocetto, Alexander, OSFS. "An Introduction to Salesian Anthropology." Vol. 6, No. 3, pp. 36-62.
>
> Reese, James M., OSFS. "Pauline Influence in the Treatise on the Love of God." Vol. 3, No. 2, pp. 5-12.
>
> Stopp, Elisabeth. "Saint Francis de Sales at Clermont College." Vol. 6, No. 1, pp. 42-63.

Stella, Pietro. *Don Bosco: Life and Work.* Translated by John Drury. 2nd revised edition. New Rochelle, NY: Don Bosco Publications, 1985.

Stopp, Elisabeth, ed. *Saint Francis de Sales: A Testimony by Saint Chantal.* Hyattsville, MD: Institute of Salesian Studies, 1967.

Wenzel, Sister Joanna Marie, VHM. *In the Midst of the World.* Brooklyn: Sisters of the Visitation, 1985.

Wright, Wendy. *Bond of Perfection.* Mahway, NJ: Paulist Press, 1985.

Index

Albera, Don Paul, 8-9, 13-14, 72, 76-77, 103-105, 110
Alimonda, Cardinal Cajetan, 54, 82
Ancina, Blessed Juvenal, 15
Annecy, 91-92, 112
Annual meetings, 83, 111-112
Apostolate of the press, 35-37
Approval of Salesian Society, 83-84
Aquinas, St. Thomas, 73
Aubry, Joseph, 39
Auffray, Fr. Augustine, 60-61
Augustine, St., 73
Aviat, Mother Francis de Sales, 119
Ayers, Fr. John, 45-47, 77-78, 110-115

Barberis, Fr. Julius, 15, 25, 87, 113
Barolo, Marchioness, 28-29, 46, 95
Beckx, Fr. Peter, 55-56
Black Madonna, 92-93, 112
Bonetti, Fr. John, 4, 47
Borel, Fr. John, 29, 30, 32, 46
Borromeo, St. Charles, 15, 18, 25
Brisson, Fr. Louis, 119-121, 123
Burton, Katherine, 119-121

Cafasso, St. Joseph, 6, 19-20, 24, 28, 30, 46
Cagliero, Cardinal John, 19-20, 64
Camus, Jean Pierre, 6, 71, 74
Carré, Ven. Caroline, 122
Caviglia, Fr. Albert, 8, 61, 74
Cavour, Camillo, 17
Ceria, Fr. Eugene, 39, 41, 60, 62, 106

Chantal, St. Jane Frances de, 6, 14, 52, 85, 105
Chappuis, Ven. Mary de Sales, 119
Chaumont, L'Abbé Henri, 122-123
Constitutions of the Salesian Society, 3, 7, 12, 41, 50, 54, 75, 107
Convitto, 18-20, 29, 46
Costamagna, Bishop James, 16, 62, 110

Da mihi animas!, 5-6, 12, 47
Daughters of Mary Help of Christians, 42-43
Daughters of St. Francis de Sales, 122
Don Bosco
    adopts the name Salesian, 40-41, 46
    an "American" Saint, 74-75
    at Chieri, 18, 23-24, 45
    at the *Convitto*, 18-19, 29, 46
    at the Oratory, 27-29, 46
    at the Rifugio, 28-29, 46
    begins his work, 26, 28
    circulates writings of St. Francis de Sales, 87-89
    death of, 95-100
    devoted to pope, 58-59, 66-67, 101, 108
    different from Francis de Sales, 10-11
    dreams of, 7, 21-22, 42, 55, 95-96, 112
    esteem for Fr. Cafasso, 19
    humanism of, 50-51
    humility of, 56
    imitation of St. Francis de Sales, 1, 3, 9-10,

imitation of *(continued)*
26-30, 38-42, 50-59,
62-63, 70-76, 93
inspired by St. Francis
de Sales, 3-10, 13,
25-27, 42, 50- 59, 97,
103, 110
living example of St.
Francis de Sales, 3, 12,
41, 56, 58, 95, 98, 103,
106
motto of, 5-6, 12, 47
not dependent on St.
Francis de Sales, 9-10
Preventive System of,
61-64, 72, 110, 114
profile of St. Francis de
Sales, 1-2
resolutions at first Mass,
24-25, 91
similarity with Francis
de Sales, 11-13, 49-59,
63-68, 93, 104-105,
109-110
spirit of, 49, chapters 8
and 9, passim
work and prayer, 75-76
writer, 1-4, 35-37

Echernier, Claudine, 118
Ecstasy of action, 53-54, 110

Favini, Don Guido, 63-64,
81-82
Francis de Sales, St.
celebration of feast of,
79-82
characteristics of, 11-13,
28-29, 46, 56-59
chosen as patron, 8, 10,
20-45, 103
cosmopolitan patron,
chapters 14 and 15
counsels of, 43-44
devoted to pope, 58-59,
66-67, 101, 108
Doctor of the Church,
89-91, 106

Don Bosco's chapel and
church of, 31-32
humanism of, 12, 50-51,
68, 86
humility of, 56
influence in English-
speaking world,
124-125
influence in Piedmont,
16-20, 45
meetings in honor of,
83-86
method of prayer, 70-71
motto, Live Jesus!, 121
nationality of, 14-16
patron at Don Bosco's
death, 95-100
profile of his life, 1-2
Rule of Life, 113
spirit of, 10-13, 23, 35-36,
43, 49, 59-68
spirituality of, 23, 68-76
union in honor of, 33,
37-38, 44-45, 123, 126
writings about, 1-5
writings of, 2-4, 9, 16,
50-51, 113-115
Fransalians. *See* Missionaries
of St. Francis de Sales
Fransoni, Archbishop Louis,
34

General Chapter Twenty, 51,
67-68, 77, 102
Giraudi, Fr. Fedele, 32
Good Shepherd, method of,
67-68
Guala, Fr. Aloysius, 18

Hermans, Francis, 76
Holiness, universal call to,
51-53
Humanism, 12, 50-51, 68, 86
Humility of the two saints,
56-57

John Baptist de la Salle, St.,
123-124